Step-by-Step Classic Kitchen

Hors d'oeuvre

A hundred graded recipes with kitchen hints and wine guide

Wordsworth Editions

Hors d'oeuvre

The purpose of this book is to help you to choose a starter for your meal. You can choose something simple or something elaborate: something for every day or for that special occasion.

The right hors d'oeuvre will excite the appetites of your family and your guests, and, together with the following courses, make a well-balanced meal. Presented with care and taste, the hors d'oeuvre will delight the eye as well as the palate. But do make sure that the one you choose allows the main course to be the star of the show. With this in mind, keep the hors d'oeuvre light and delicate, and make sure it complements what is to follow: it would never do to begin with a soufflé if the main course is an egg dish; to start with crudités if your main course is accompanied by several salads, or to begin with a vol-au-vent and serve apple pie for dessert.

For a light lunch, a buffet, or a family meal in front of the television, a selection of several of the hors d'oeuvre you will find in this volume makes an excellent meal: an iced soup; finely sliced vegetables, raw or cooked, served with various sauces and pickles; savoury tartlets and assorted canapés of meat or fish; followed by a simple dessert.

However, for the traditional full-course meal, the hors d'oeuvre should be more elaborate: seafood in puff pastry, a vol-au-vent, something in aspic, or an unexpected salad of exotic fruits or rare fish.

Preparing some of these hors d'oeuvre undoubtedly requires much time and effort, but most can be prepared well in advance, allowing you to spend more time relaxing with your guests and your family, and to enjoy the meal as much as they do.

Table of Contents

Notes: Getting the Best out of this Book

1. The preparation times given in the Table of Contents and with each recipe are minimum times: they will vary according to the cook's ability and the equipment available. Certain of the recipes require periods for marinading or chilling. These have not been taken into account in the times given in the table, but are indicated at the head of each recipe.

2. At the bottom of certain pages, you will find some useful pieces of information and advice, and the following recipes: Smoked fish canapés (page 6), Mayonnaise (20), Melon with port (22), Melon mousse (22), Aioli (34), Fish sauces (36), Jellied fish stock (49), Stuffed pancakes (77).

3. It is always best to use red or white wine vinegar in the recipes where vinegar is required; the results will not be the same if you use malt vinegar. In the same way, freshly ground black pepper should always be used in preference to ready-ground pepper.

4. Certain of the recipes require cooking au bain-marie. This consists of placing whatever is to be cooked in a saucepan inside a larger saucepan filled with almost-boiling water. This method is ideal for cooking certain delicate sauces or other dishes which would react badly if exposed to a direct heat.

5. Oven temperatures. The following are Gas, Fahrenheit and Centigrade equivalents:

Gas	¼	½	1	2	3	4	5	6	7	8	9
°F	225	250	275	300	325	350	375	400	425	450	475
°C	110	120	140	160	170	180	190	200	220	230	250

6. It is important when using these recipes to follow the exact proportions. A set of kitchen scales, measuring jug, glass and spoons are essential. Follow either metric or avoirdupois measurements in each recipe.

7. To help you choose the right wine for your meal, see page 80.

Canapés aux Bouquets

Serves 3-6. Preparation and cooking: 15 min

Prawn Canapés

★

○ **6 slices white bread, crusts removed**
○ **200g (7 oz) prawns**
○ **60ml (4 tbls) mayonnaise**
○ **6 slices Cheshire cheese**

1. Put aside 12 of the nicest prawns. Shell and finely chop the rest.
2. In a bowl, mix the minced prawns and mayonnaise.
3. Toast the slices of bread on both sides. Spread the prawn mayonnaise on them and cover with a slice of cheese.
4. Place in an ovenproof dish and leave under the grill until the cheese starts to melt. Remove and garnish each canapé with 2 prawns. Serve at once.

Canapés aux Champignons

Serves 5-10. Preparation and cooking: 20 min

Mushroom Canapés

★

○ **10 slices white bread, crusts removed**
○ **250g (9 oz) button mushrooms**
○ **100ml (3½ fl oz) double cream**
○ **100g (4 oz) Gruyère cheese**
○ **1 slice smoked ham (Parma or Bayonne style)**
○ **juice of 1 lemon**
○ **15 sprigs chervil, coarsely chopped**
○ **2 pinches grated nutmeg**
○ **salt and pepper**

1. Remove the earthy base of the mushrooms and wash, dry and slice them.
2. Dice the ham and cheese. Place the sliced mushrooms in a bowl and pour the lemon juice over them. Add the cream, ham and cheese, chervil, grated nutmeg, and salt and pepper to taste. Mix well.
3. Toast the bread on both sides. Arrange on a dish and spread the mushroom mixture on each slice while they are still hot. Serve at once.

Canapés aux Moules

Serves 5-10. Preparation and cooking: 20 min

Mussel Canapés

★

○ **10 slices white bread, crusts removed**
○ **20 large mussels**
○ **60ml (4 tbls) mayonnaise**
○ **1 onion, chopped**
○ **1 small handful fresh parsley, chervil, tarragon and chives, chopped**
○ **30ml (2 tbls) capers**
○ **pepper**

1. Scrape the mussels and scrub them well. Wash under running water. Put them in a pan over a high heat for 5 minutes or until they open. Drain them, and discard the shells.
2. Mix mayonnaise, chopped onion, herbs and capers, and season with pepper to taste. Mix well.
3. Toast the bread on each side. Leave to cool.
4. Spread the mayonnaise mixture on the bread and garnish each canapé with 2 mussels.

Smoked fish canapés are delicious. Use eel, herring, salmon or sturgeon, on black or rye bread. With a fork, mix some chopped chervil into some Petit-suisse (soft cream cheese) or fromage blanc (which you can buy in certain good delicatessens). Season with salt and pepper. Spread this on the slices of bread. Garnish with thin slices of smoked eel or smoked herring and a slice of cucumber. Serve with dried fruit (raisins, figs, prunes, etc) to create a pleasant contrast.

Canapés au Cresson et aux Radis

Serves 5-10. Preparation and cooking: 20 min

Watercress and Radish Canapés

- ○ **10 slices bread (from a cottage loaf), crusts removed**
- ○ **1 bunch watercress**
- ○ **1 bunch red radishes**
- ○ **60ml (4 tbls) mayonnaise**
- ○ **15 sprigs chervil, coarsely chopped**

1. Trim the watercress to just below the point where the leaves join the stems. Wash and drain the leaves, then chop finely.
2. Add the chopped watercress and chervil to the mayonnaise and mix well.
3. Trim the radishes. Wash and slice.
4. Toast the bread on each side and leave to cool. Spread the mayonnaise mixture thickly on each slice. Garnish with slices of radish around the edge of each canapé.

Canapés au Jambon et aux Cèpes

Serves 5-10. Preparation and cooking: 20 min

Ham and Mushroom Canapés

★

- ○ **10 slices white bread, crusts removed**
- ○ **100g (4 oz) softened butter**
- ○ **4 slices cooked ham**
- ○ **4 shallots**
- ○ **1 tin cèpes (200g/7 oz) or 100g (4 oz) fresh mushrooms**
- ○ **salt and pepper**

1. Cut one slice of ham into 10 small diamond shaped pieces and mince the remainder.
2. Peel and chop the shallots.
3. Put the butter, shallots and minced ham in a bowl. Season with salt and pepper to taste and mix well with a fork.
4. Drain and slice the cèpes. (Alternatively, sauté the fresh mushrooms lightly in butter.) Toast the slices of bread on both sides. Leave to cool.
5. Spread a thick layer of the ham and butter mixture onto the slices of bread. Garnish each one with slices of cèpe or mushroom and pieces of ham.

Canapés au Gruyère et au Concombre

Serves 5-10. Preparation and cooking: 20 min

Cucumber and Gruyère Canapés

★

- ○ **10 slices bread (from cottage loaf), crusts removed**
- ○ **1 clove garlic**
- ○ **200g (7 oz) Gruyère cheese**
- ○ **30ml (2 tbls) olive oil**
- ○ **½ cucumber, peeled and seeded**
- ○ **10 rolled anchovy fillets, drained**

1. Peel the garlic, cut in half and rub on each slice of bread.
2. Heat the oil in a frying pan and fry the bread on both sides. Drain on absorbent paper.
3. Slice the cucumber and grate the cheese.
4. Cover each slice of bread with cheese and grill until the cheese starts to melt.
5. Place the canapés on a serving dish, garnish with cucumber slices and anchovy fillets. Serve at once.

Canapés are thin slices of fresh, fried or toasted bread covered with a variety of savoury mixtures. To make them look more attractive, the bread may be cut into many different shapes and sizes: round, square, triangular, etc.

You can use many kinds of bread: black, wholemeal, rye, brown, white, etc, and these can be spread with butter mixed with a variety of flavourings: butter with lemon, tarragon, tomato, or mustard, for example. Then garnish with any number of mixtures using vegetables, fish, poultry, cold meat, cheese, egg . . . just use your imagination!

Canapés à la Tapenade

Serves 5-10. Preparation and cooking: 20 min

Anchovy Paste Canapés

★

○ **10 slices bread (from a cottage loaf), crusts removed**
○ **1 small green pepper**
○ **200g (7 oz) large black olives**
○ **100g (4 oz) anchovy fillets in oil**
○ **30ml (2 tbls) capers**
○ **60ml (4 tbls) olive oil**
○ **juice of 1 lemon**
○ **pepper**

1. Stone the olives.
2. Mash the olives, anchovy fillets and capers. Add the olive oil, a little at a time, along with the lemon juice, until you have a thick sauce. Season with pepper to taste and refrigerate.
3. Cut the pepper in half, discard the seeds and cut into thin strips.
4. Toast the bread on both sides. Spread the sauce on the hot toast and garnish with the strips of pepper.

Canapés aux Anchois

Serves 4. Preparation and cooking: 15 min

Anchovy Canapés

★

○ **4 slices white bread, crusts removed**
○ **2 small tins anchovies in oil (50g/2 oz each)**
○ **10 radishes**
○ **3 sprigs parsley, roughly chopped**
○ **3 hard-boiled eggs**
○ **pepper**

1. Cut each slice of bread into 2 triangles.
2. Shell and slice the eggs. Wash, trim and slice the radishes.
3. Put the anchovies with their oil in a saucepan. Leave them to melt over a low heat, stirring with a wooden spoon, until they take on the consistency of a paste. Remove from the heat and season lightly with pepper.
4. Toast the bread on both sides and spread with anchovy paste. Garnish with the slices of egg and radish and sprinkle with parsley. Serve at once.

Canapés à l'Ail et aux Oeufs

Serves 2-4. Preparation and cooking: 15 min

Egg and Garlic Canapés

★

○ **4 slices wholemeal bread, crusts removed**
○ **4 eggs**
○ **1 clove garlic**
○ **15ml (1 tbls) olive oil**
○ **20 black olives**
○ **salt and pepper**

1. Stone the olives and mince them as finely as possible. Peel the garlic, cut in half and rub on each slice of bread. Fry the bread in oil for 2 minutes on each side.
2. Prepare a *bain-marie*. In the small saucepan break the eggs and stir with a wooden spoon (as if making scrambled eggs). (This method, *au bain-marie*, is used so that the mixture remains smooth.) Season with salt and pepper. Top each slice of fried bread with the egg mixture and place the minced olives on top.

Canapés aux Pointes d'Asperges

Serves 5-10. Preparation and cooking: 10 min

Asparagus Canapés

★

○ **10 slices rye bread, crusts removed**
○ **100g (4 oz) tin asparagus tips**
○ **50g (2 oz) butter**
○ **100g (4 oz) grated Gruyère cheese**

1. Open the tin of asparagus tips and drain. Toast the slices of bread on both sides and butter them while still hot.
2. Garnish each slice with asparagus tips. Sprinkle with the grated cheese. Put the slices of bread under the grill until the cheese starts to melt. Serve at once.

Brochettes de Pruneaux

Serves 4. Preparation: 10 min Cooking: 45 min

Grilled Prunes on Skewers

★★

○ **500g (18 oz) leeks**
○ **200g (7 oz) prunes, soaked overnight in cold water**
○ **325g (11 oz) smoked bacon**
○ **24 small onions or pickling onions**

For the sauce:
○ **15ml (1 tbls) honey**
○ **15 ml (1 tbls) soya sauce**
○ **2 cloves**
○ **30ml (2 tbls) ketchup or tomato sauce**
○ **30ml (2 tbls) white wine**
○ **salt and pepper**

1. Drain and stone the prunes. Put aside.
2. Wash the leeks and discard roots and green tops. Cook in salted water for 20 minutes, or 10 minutes in a pressure cooker. Drain well (press between your hands to remove excess water) and leave to cool, then cut into chunks.
3. Discard the bacon rind, and dice the bacon into about 24 small pieces.
4. Peel the onions.
5. Place the ingredients for the sauce in a saucepan. Cook, uncovered, over a high heat. After about 15 minutes the sauce should be thick. Remove from heat.
6. Thread on skewers alternate pieces of prune, bacon, onion and leek.
7. Cook the kebabs under the grill for at least 10 minutes or until cooked. Turn frequently and baste with the sauce. Serve at once.

Brochettes d'Escargots

Serves 4-8. Preparation: 20 min Cooking: 1 hr 10 min

Grilled Snails on Skewers

★★

○ **4 dozen snails (in their shells if available, otherwise a tin of 48 snails)**
○ **50g (2 oz) butter**
○ **4 shallots**
○ **small bunch chives, chopped**
○ **200g (7 oz) smoked bacon**
○ **25g (1 oz) breadcrumbs**
○ **45ml (3 tbls) coarse salt**
○ **salt and pepper**

For the court-bouillon:
○ **1 bouquet garni consisting of: 1 sprig of thyme, 2 bay leaves, 3 sprigs parsley**
○ **1 clove garlic**
○ **2 small carrots, sliced**
○ **10 whole peppercorns**
○ **coarse salt**

1. If you are using snails in their shells: sprinkle the snails with 3 tbls of coarse salt and leave to soak for 2 hours. Wash well under running water.
2. Prepare the stock: in a large saucepan filled with water, put the bouquet garni, carrots, garlic, salt and peppercorns. Add the snails and cook for 1 hour over medium heat. Remove the snails from the stock and leave to cool. Then remove from their shells and discard the black end.
3. If you are using snails from a tin, cook them in the stock for only 10 minutes. Discard the bacon rind, and cut the bacon into approximately 24 small pieces. Peel the shallots and chop finely. In a bowl, mix the butter, shallots and chives; season.
4. Thread snails onto skewers, alternating with the pieces of bacon.
5. Place the breadcrumbs on a plate. Heat the shallot butter, but do not allow to boil. Dip the kebabs into it, then turn them in the breadcrumbs. Cook under the grill for 5 minutes on each side, basting with the shallot butter. Serve hot.

Kebabs or brochettes are chunks of meat, fish, fruit or vegetables threaded on skewers, cooked over charcoal or under the grill.

Kebabs are an original and amusing way of cooking vegetables: you can use pieces of onion, pepper, tomato, fennel, celery, red cabbage or mushrooms, for example, in whatever combinations you choose. If you like sweet and sour tastes, squares of apple, pineapple or fig make the kebabs even more interesting!

Cornets de Jambon (p16) ▶

Brochettes de Jambon et de Pruneaux

Bacon and Prune Kebabs

Serves 5. Preparation: 15 min Cooking: 5 min

★

○ **20 thin slices smoked bacon**
○ **40 prunes, soaked overnight in cold water**

1. Drain and stone the prunes.
2. Wrap 2 prunes in each slice of bacon. Thread 4 slices of bacon on each skewer.
3. Grill the kebabs for 5 minutes, turning frequently. Serve at once.

These kebabs can be served with a mint sauce: mix 15cl (5 fl oz) yogurt with 30ml (2 tbls) double cream. Add a pinch of paprika, about 20 finely chopped mint leaves and salt and pepper to taste.

Brochettes de Lotte

Monkfish Kebabs

Serves 6. Preparation: 15 min Cooking: 15 min

★★

○ **1kg (2¼ lb) monkfish**
○ **30 slices smoked bacon**
○ **20 black olives, stoned**
○ **3 sprigs thyme**
○ **1 lemon**
○ **pepper**

1. Discard bones and skin, and cut the fish into small pieces.
2. Wrap each piece of fish in 1 or 2 slices of bacon, and season with pepper. Thread 4 of these small packets onto each skewer, alternating with black olives. Sprinkle with thyme leaves.
3. Cook under the grill for 10 to 15 minutes. Serve hot with slices of lemon.

Boulettes de Viande

Meatballs

Serves 6. Preparation: 30 min Cooking: 20 min

★★

○ **500g (18 oz) minced steak**
○ **2 small onions**
○ **30g (1¼ oz) breadcrumbs**
○ **1 egg**
○ **15ml (1 tbls) parsley, coarsely chopped**
○ **15ml (1 tbls) mint leaves, coarsely chopped**
○ **60ml (4 tbls) white wine**
○ **45ml (3 tbls) oil**
○ **20g (¾ oz) butter**
○ **flour**
○ **salt and pepper**

1. Peel the onions, slice thinly, and sauté in the butter over a low heat for 10 minutes.
2. Using a fork, blend the minced meat with the chopped parsley, mint, egg, breadcrumbs and salt and pepper. Add the onions and mix once again.
3. Make walnut-size meatballs: you should end up with approximately 30. Roll each one in flour.
4. Heat the oil in a frying pan until very hot, then fry the meatballs on all sides.
5. Remove when brown and discard the cooking oil. Put the meatballs back in the frying pan and pour over the wine. Cook for 5 minutes. Serve at once.

These meatballs can be served on skewers, alternating with diced tomatoes and slices of raw onion.

You can make kebabs that are not cooked. Try thin slices of ham (Parma or Bayonne style) or smoked meat, wrapped around fresh or dried fruit (whole or cut into pieces), alternating with diced Gruyère cheese.

Oeufs Farcis aux Cèpes

Serves 3-6. Preparation: 10 min Cooking: 30 min

Eggs Stuffed with Mushrooms

★★

○ 3 eggs
○ 1 tin of cèpes (120g/4½ oz) or 50g (2 oz) fresh mushrooms
○ 1 clove garlic
○ 15ml (1 tbls) parsley and chives, chopped
○ 100ml (3½ fl oz) double cream
○ 30g (1¼ oz) butter
○ salt and pepper

1. Preheat the oven to 250°C (475°F; gas mark 9).
2. Hard boil the eggs.
3. If using tinned cèpes, drain them and chop finely. Otherwise wash, trim and chop the mushrooms. Peel and crush the garlic. In a frying pan, melt the butter over a low heat; add the mushrooms, garlic, chopped chives and parsley. Season. Cook for 15 minutes, stirring frequently with a wooden spoon. Remove from heat.
4. Shell the eggs. Halve them, keeping the white intact. Remove the yolks and mash with a fork.
5. Blend the cream with the egg yolks; add the mushrooms. Mix once more. Fill the halved egg whites with this mixture and place in the preheated oven for a few minutes until they are just beginning to brown.

Oeufs Frits au Vin

Serves 6. Preparation: 25 min Cooking: 30 min

Fried Eggs on Toast with Wine Sauce

★★

○ 6 eggs
○ 6 slices white bread
○ 1 clove garlic
○ 30ml (2 tbls) oil
○ 30g (1 oz) butter
○ salt and pepper

For the sauce:
○ 240ml (9 fl oz) red wine
○ 5 small white onions (or pickling onions), minced
○ 1 slice smoked ham (Parma or Bayonne style), diced
○ 15ml (1 tbls) flour
○ 1 sprig thyme
○ 2 bay leaves
○ white part of 1 leek, cut into slices
○ 20g (¾ oz) butter
○ salt and pepper

1. First prepare the sauce. Pour the wine into a small saucepan, place over a high heat and set alight; when the flame dies down, remove from heat.
2. Melt the butter in a frying pan. Fry the onions and leek. Add the diced ham, thyme and bay leaves. Sprinkle on the flour. When the ingredients start to brown, pour over the wine. Season with salt and pepper and simmer for 20 minutes.
3. Peel the garlic, cut in half and rub it on the slices of bread. Fry the bread in the oil on both sides. Remove from heat, place on a serving dish and keep warm.
4. Fry the eggs in butter, basting the yolks with a spoon to make sure they are well cooked. Season. When the eggs are fried, place them on the slices of bread. Remove the thyme and bay leaves from the sauce and pour around the toast. Serve immediately.

Oeufs Bonne Femme

Serves 4. Preparation: 10 min Cooking: 10 min

Baked Eggs with Cream and Tarragon

★

○ 4 eggs
○ 1 sprig tarragon
○ 200ml (7 fl oz) double cream
○ 20g (¾ oz) butter
○ salt and pepper

1. Wash and dry the tarragon and remove the leaves.
2. Preheat the oven to 200°C (400°F; gas mark 6).
3. Butter the bottom and sides of 4 small ovenproof ramekins or cocotte dishes. Place a few tarragon leaves at the bottom and on the sides of each dish. Pour 15ml (1 tbls) cream in each dish, then break one egg into each dish. Cover with another 15ml (1 tbls) of cream. Season and garnish with more tarragon leaves.
4. Place the ramekins in a large ovenproof dish filled with water and cook for 10 minutes. Serve at once.

Oeufs Brouillés à l'Oseille

Serves 4-6. Preparation: 10 min Cooking: 20 min

Scrambled Eggs with Sorrel

★★

○ **8 eggs**
○ **40 sorrel leaves**
○ **15ml (1 tbls) double cream**
○ **20g (¾ oz) butter**
○ **a few fresh tarragon leaves**
○ **salt and pepper**

1. Wash the sorrel leaves thoroughly under running water. Remove the stalks.
2. Melt the butter in a small saucepan over a medium heat. When it starts to froth, add the sorrel leaves. Cook, stirring occasionally, for 10 minutes.
3. Remove the saucepan from the heat and add the eggs. Place this into a larger saucepan filled with water and cook for a further 10 minutes, scrambling the eggs with the sorrel. When the mixture is cooked, remove from heat.
4. Season with 3 pinches of salt and some pepper. Bind with the cream, which reduces the bitterness of the sorrel. Add the finely chopped tarragon.

Serve with slices of toasted white or rye bread.

Pâté d'Oeufs

Serves 4-6. Preparation: 15 min Cooking: 25 min

Egg and Potato Purée

○ **8 potatoes**
○ **4 eggs**
○ **15ml (1 tbls) groundnut oil**
○ **15 sprigs parsley, coarsely chopped**
○ **salt and pepper**

1. Wash the potatoes. Cook unpeeled in salted water for 25 minutes.
2. Meanwhile, hard boil the eggs, drain and shell them.
3. In a bowl, mash the eggs thoroughly with a fork.
4. Drain and peel the cooked potatoes. Add to the eggs, and continue mashing, blending in the oil and chopped parsley. Season. Form the mixture into a round 2 to 3cm (about 1 inch) thick. Serve cold.

Oeufs Pochés en Sauce

Serves 2-4. Preparation: 10 min Cooking: 25 min

Poached Eggs in Mustard and White Wine Sauce

★★

○ **4 eggs**
○ **30ml (2 tbls) vinegar**

For the sauce:
○ **2 shallots**
○ **30g (1¼ oz) flour**
○ **60ml (2 fl oz) white wine**
○ **15ml (1 tbls) French mustard**
○ **120ml (4 fl oz) chicken stock**
○ **30g (1¼ oz) butter**
○ **salt and pepper**

1. Peel and chop the shallots.
2. Melt the butter in a frying pan. Add the shallots, then the flour. When they start to brown, moisten with the wine and stock. Season with salt and pepper and simmer for 20 minutes.
3. Shortly before the sauce is finished, bring 2 litres (approx 3½ pints) of water and the vinegar to the boil. To poach the eggs, break them over the surface of the water. Reduce the heat and simmer for 4 minutes. Remove the eggs with a skimmer and place on a serving dish.
4. Add mustard to the sauce and mix well. Remove from the heat and pour over the eggs. Serve at once.

Poached eggs are delicious with soups: just break the egg directly into the hot soup.

Avocats aux Fruits (p17) ▶

Cornets de Jambon

Serves 4. Preparation: 15 min Cooking: 30 min

Ham Cornets Filled with Vegetable Mayonnaise

★★

○ **200g (7 oz) rice**
○ **100g (4 oz) peas**
○ **100g (4 oz) French beans**
○ **2 turnips**
○ **2 carrots**
○ **100g (4 oz) Emmenthal cheese**
○ **4 slices cooked ham**
○ **90ml (6 tbls) mayonnaise**
○ **lettuce leaves**
○ **2 tomatoes**
○ **10 sprigs parsley**
○ **salt and pepper**

1. Cook the rice in boiling water for 15 minutes or until tender. Drain and rinse under hot running water.
2. While the rice is cooking, shell the peas; wash, top, tail and dice the French beans; peel and dice the turnips and carrots. Cook the vegetables for 15 minutes (10 minutes in a pressure cooker) in boiling salted water. They should still be crisp. Drain.
3. Dice the cheese. In a bowl, mix together the vegetables, rice, mayonnaise and cheese. Season to taste.
4. Lay a slice of ham on a dish, spoon a quarter of the vegetable mixture down the centre and roll up. Repeat with the remaining slices of ham. Place some lettuce leaves on a serving dish and top with ham cornets. Garnish with halved tomatoes sprinkled with parsley.

Pamplemousses Farcis

Serves 4. Preparation 15 min

Stuffed Grapefruit

★

○ **2 grapefruit**
○ **juice of 1 orange**
○ **150g (5 oz) prawns**
○ **1 avocado**

For the sauce:
○ **30ml (2 tbls) ketchup**
○ **50ml (3 heaped tbls) mayonnaise**
○ **pinch sugar**
○ **pinch paprika**

1. Halve the grapefruit. Scoop out the flesh, being careful not to break the skin. Put the shells aside. Remove the white skin from the segments and dice the flesh. Halve the avocado, remove the stone, scoop out the flesh and dice it finely.
2. Mix the grapefruit, avocado and orange juice in a bowl.
3. Shell the prawns and add them to the fruit.
4. Mix together the ingredients for the sauce, add to the grapefruit mixture and fill the shells. Chill in the refrigerator until ready to serve.

Avocats Piquants

Serves 4. Preparation: 15 min

Avocados Stuffed with Devilled Crab

★★

○ **2 large avocados**
○ **1 tin (150g/5 oz) crabmeat**
○ **100g (4 oz) prawns**
○ **4 large mushrooms**
○ **30ml (2 tbls) double cream**
○ **45ml (3 tbls) mayonnaise**
○ **juice of 1 lemon**
○ **6 drops Tabasco sauce**
○ **4 sprigs parsley, chopped**
○ **salt**

1. Halve the avocados and discard the stones. Carefully scoop out the flesh, keeping the skins intact, and dice finely. Reserve the avocado skins.
2. Drain the crabmeat, removing any cartilage, and flake. Shell the prawns. Trim the mushrooms, wash, and slice thinly. Mix with the crabmeat and prawns in a bowl, add the avocado and mix well.
3. In a small bowl, mix the cream with 30ml (2 tbls) mayonnaise. When well blended, add another tablespoon of mayonnaise, the lemon juice and Tabasco sauce. Season with salt and combine with the crabmeat mixture.
4. Fill each avocado skin and garnish with the chopped parsley. Serve chilled.

Avocats aux Fruits

Serves 4. Preparation: 10 min

Avocados Stuffed with Fruit

★

- ○ **2 avocados**
- ○ **50g (2 oz) prawns**
- ○ **juice of ½ orange**
- ○ **1 apple**
- ○ **1 lemon**
- ○ **100ml (3½ fl oz) double cream**
- ○ **2 sprigs parsley**
- ○ **salt and pepper**

1. Shell and mince the prawns. Peel the apple and cut into small pieces. Wash and chop the parsley.
2. To prepare the sauce, mix the orange juice with the cream and season with salt and pepper. Add the diced apple and prawns. Mix well.
3. Halve the avocados and remove the stones. Spoon the prawn mixture into the centres. Garnish with lemon wedges and chopped parsley.

Avocats au Crabe

Serves 4. Preparation: 10 min

Avocados with Crab

★

- ○ **2 avocados**
- ○ **1 tin (150g/5 oz) crabmeat**
- ○ **45ml (3 tbls) mayonnaise**
- ○ **juice of 1 lemon**
- ○ **15ml (1 tbls) ketchup**

1. Halve the avocados. Discard the stones.
2. Mix together the mayonnaise, lemon juice and ketchup. Blend well.
3. Drain the crab, remove any cartilage, flake and add to the sauce. Mix well.
4. Spoon into the avocados. Serve chilled.

Avocats Arméniens

Serves 4. Preparation: 10 min

Avocados Armenian Style

★★

- ○ **2 avocados**
- ○ **10g (½ oz) smoked cod's roe**
- ○ **30ml (2 tbls) double cream**
- ○ **juice of 1 lemon**
- ○ **pepper**

1. Halve the avocados and remove the stones. Scoop out the flesh and dice. Sprinkle with some of the lemon juice. Put aside, with the avocado skins.
2. Bring a large saucepan of water to the boil. Dip the cod's roe into the water for a few minutes and remove the skin.
3. In a bowl, blend the cream into the roe and season with pepper. Add the avocado flesh together with the rest of the lemon juice. Mix well.
4. Fill each avocado skin with the mixture. Serve chilled.

Feuilles de Chou Farcies aux Légumes

Serves 4. Preparation: 20 min Cooking: 35 min

Stuffed Cabbage Leaves

★★

- ○ **10 white cabbage leaves**
- ○ **2 carrots, cut into strips**
- ○ **3 leeks, white part only, cut into slices**
- ○ **10 small pieces smoked bacon**
- ○ **1 green pepper, cut into small strips**
- ○ **150g (5 oz) grated Gruyère cheese**
- ○ **150g (5 oz) butter**
- ○ **salt and pepper**

1. Wash the cabbage leaves. Blanch in boiling salted water for 15 minutes. Drain and put aside 8 leaves. Cut the 2 remaining leaves into strips.
2. In a saucepan, brown the cabbage strips, carrots, leeks and pepper in 100g (4 oz) butter. Cook for 20 minutes, adding a little water from time to time. Season.
3. Spread out the cabbage leaves and put 30ml (2 tbls) of the vegetable stuffing on each, roll the leaves and fold over to make small parcels. Melt the remaining butter in a flameproof casserole, and brown the cabbage leaves and bacon for 15 minutes. Sprinkle with the grated cheese before serving.

Artichauts aux Bouquets

Serves 4. Preparation: 15 min Cooking: 35 min

Artichokes with Prawns

★ ★

- ○ **4 artichokes**
- ○ **juice of 3 lemons**
- ○ **200g (7 oz) prawns**
- ○ **15 sprigs chervil**
- ○ **200ml (7 fl oz) double cream**
- ○ **20g (¾ oz) butter**
- ○ **salt and pepper**

1. Cut off the stalks of the artichokes. Trim about 1cm (less than ½ in) off the ends of leaves. Wash well under cold running water, spreading the leaves slightly.
2. Bring to the boil a large saucepan of water and the juice of 2 lemons. Add the artichokes and cook for 30 minutes. Drain and leave to cool.
3. Meanwhile, shell the prawns. Put aside. Squeeze the juice from the remaining lemon. Wash the chervil and chop finely.
4. When the artichokes have cooled, spread the top leaves, pull the inside leaves out and, using a teaspoon, scrape away the hairy choke. Put aside.
5. Melt the butter in a frying pan. Add the cream and stir until it starts to boil. Add the remaining lemon juice. This should result in a frothy sauce. Then add the prawns and chopped chervil. Season with salt and pepper. Leave to cook for a further 2 minutes.
6. Fill each artichoke with the mixture and serve at once.

For a heartier dish, serve this over boiled white rice.

Concombres Farcis

Serves 4. Preparation: 10 min Cooking: 35 min

Stuffed Cucumbers

★ ★

- ○ **2 cucumbers**
- ○ **½ head fennel**
- ○ **1 small green pepper**
- ○ **3 stalks chard**
- ○ **1 mozzarella cheese (about 175g/6 oz)**
- ○ **50g (2 oz) flaked almonds**
- ○ **5 sprigs fresh mint**
- ○ **coarse salt**
- ○ **juice of 1 lemon**
- ○ **30g (1¼ oz) butter**
- ○ **salt and pepper**

1. Peel the cucumbers, cut off the ends, and halve lengthways. Scoop out the seeds and discard.
2. Prepare the vegetables: wash the chard and fennel; wash the pepper and discard the seeds. Cut the vegetables into pieces and steam them for 20 minutes (10 minutes if using a pressure cooker).
3. Melt 20g (¾ oz) butter in a frying pan over a medium heat. Brown the chard, fennel and green pepper for 5 minutes. Reduce the heat. Add the remaining butter to the frying pan and sprinkle in the almonds. Fry gently until they are beginning to brown. Then add the finely chopped mint leaves. Season with salt and pepper and mix well.
4. On chopping board roughly chop the contents of the frying pan. Meanwhile, bring to the boil a large saucepan of water, and add 2 pinches of coarse salt.
5. Blanch the cucumbers in boiling water for 5 minutes. Drain and leave to cool.
6. Stuff each cucumber with the vegetable mixture. Press the stuffing down and leave to cool. Arrange the cucumbers on a serving dish. Surround with the remaining stuffing and pour over the lemon juice. Garnish with strips of mozzarella.

Poivrons Farcis

Serves 5-10. Preparation and cooking: 1 hr 30 min

Stuffed Peppers

★★

- ○ **10 medium-sized green peppers**
- ○ **1 onion**
- ○ **1 clove garlic, chopped**
- ○ **700g (1½ lb) minced steak**
- ○ **100g (4 oz) rice**
- ○ **6 tomatoes**
- ○ **15ml (1 tbls) olive oil**
- ○ **30g (1¼ oz) breadcrumbs**
- ○ **30g (1¼ oz) butter**
- ○ **1 bunch parsley, finely chopped**
- ○ **salt and pepper**

1. Preheat the oven to 170°C (325°F; gas mark 3).
2. Bring some salted water to the boil in a large saucepan. Cut the tops off the peppers (these will be used as lids), remove the seeds and core, and wash. Blanch the peppers and lids in boiling water for 5 minutes. Remove and drain, but leave the water on the heat.
3. Plunge the tomatoes into the water for 10 seconds. Drain, peel and remove the seeds. Put aside 2 tomatoes.
4. Heat the olive oil in a frying pan. Add 4 tomatoes and mash them with a fork. Season. When the liquid from the tomatoes has evaporated, reduce the heat and simmer for 15 minutes, until the sauce thickens.
5. Peel the onion and slice thinly. In another frying pan melt 20g (¾ oz) butter over a medium heat. Sauté the onion slices for 10 minutes. Add the garlic and minced steak. With a fork, mix in the rice, chopped parsley and the 2 remaining tomatoes, chopped. Season and simmer for 5 minutes.
6. Spoon the stuffing into the peppers and cover with the lids. Place in an ovenproof dish.
7. Soften the remaining butter and combine with the breadcrumbs. Spread over the peppers. Surround the peppers with the tomato sauce. Place in the oven and cook for about 1 hour, or until tender.

Feuilles de Vigne Farcies

Serves 6. Preparation: 30 min Cooking: 1 hr 20 min

Stuffed Vine Leaves

★★★

- ○ **1 tin (500g/18 oz) vine leaves**
- ○ **150ml (10 tbls) olive oil**
- ○ **500g (18 oz) onions**
- ○ **200g (7 oz) rice**
- ○ **50g (2 oz) currants**
- ○ **30ml (2 tbls) pine nuts**
- ○ **3 lemons**
- ○ **salt and pepper**
- ○ **15 mint leaves**

1. Peel the onions and slice thinly. Heat 60ml (4 tbls) olive oil in a frying pan and brown the onions over a low heat for 10 minutes. Add the rice and cook for 5 minutes.
2. Squeeze the juice from 1 lemon. Wash and chop the mint leaves. Add the mint, lemon juice, pine nuts, currants and 45ml (3 tbls) olive oil to the rice in the frying pan. Season. Simmer for 5 minutes, then leave to cool.
3. Wash the vine leaves in cold water. (If you have been able to obtain fresh vine leaves, blanch them for 3 minutes, then drain.)
4. Spread out a leaf, shiny side downwards, and place a tablespoon of stuffing into the centre. Fold the stem end over the filling, then fold the sides towards the middle and roll up. Squeeze the rolled vine leaf lightly in your hand. Continue with the rest of the leaves in the same way.
5. Layer the stuffed leaves tightly in a flameproof casserole. Squeeze the juice from 1 lemon and pour over the vine leaves. Add 45ml (3 tbls) olive oil and 30ml (2 tbls) hot water. Put a plate over the stuffed vine leaves to prevent them from opening while cooking. Cover with a lid and simmer for 1 hour. Leave to cool in the casserole. Serve cold, garnished with the remaining lemon, sliced.

To make a mayonnaise: in a bowl, dissolve 3 pinches of salt with 5ml (1 tsp) vinegar. Add 1 egg yolk and 5ml (1 tsp) French mustard. Mix with a wooden spoon. Leave to stand for 1 to 2 minutes. Then add 100ml (3½ fl oz) of oil, a little at a time, beating continuously with a wooden spoon. Finish beating with a whisk.

Tomates Fourrées au Thon

Serves 4. Preparation: 15 min Cooking: 6 min

Tomatoes Stuffed with Tuna Fish

★★

- ○ **4 large tomatoes**
- ○ **1 slice tuna weighing 200g (7 oz)**
- ○ **4 shallots**
- ○ **100g (4 oz) prawns**
- ○ **100ml (3½ fl oz) double cream**
- ○ **30ml (2 tbls) olive oil**
- ○ **juice of 1 lemon**
- ○ **15 sprigs chervil, coarsely chopped (or substitute chopped parsley)**
- ○ **salt and pepper**

1. Slice off the top of each tomato, and carefully take out the seeds with a teaspoon. Place the tomatoes on a dish.
2. Grill the slice of tuna, turning once, for 5 to 6 minutes, brushing it with the olive oil. Then remove the skin and backbone and flake the tuna.
3. Peel the shallots and shell the prawns. Mince the shallots, prawns and tuna together. Put all the ingredients in a bowl, add the chopped chervil, cream and lemon juice. Season and mix well.
4. Fill each tomato with the filling and serve at once.

Tomates Farcies au Roquefort

Serves 6. Preparation: 10 min

Tomatoes Stuffed with Roquefort

★

- ○ **6 large tomatoes**
- ○ **100g (4 oz) fromage blanc or cream cheese**
- ○ **100g (4 oz) Roquefort cheese**
- ○ **100ml (3½ fl oz) double cream**
- ○ **10 sprigs parsley, coarsely chopped**
- ○ **salt and pepper**

1. Slice off the top of each tomato and put aside (these will be used as lids). Scoop out the flesh and seeds with a teaspoon.
2. In a bowl, blend the fromage blanc with the cream and beat with a whisk. Mash the Roquefort with a fork and add to the fromage blanc mixture. Season. Add the parsley, mix well.
3. Place the tomatoes on a serving dish and fill each one with the filling. Cover the lids and serve cold.

Escargots de Bourgogne

Serves 4-8. Preparation: 25 min Cooking: 1 hr 40 min

Snails with Garlic Butter

★★

- ○ **4 dozen snails (in their shells if available, otherwise 48 tinned snails and shells)**
- ○ **450g (1 lb) butter**
- ○ **3 cloves garlic**
- ○ **1 bunch parsley, chopped**
- ○ **coarse salt**
- ○ **salt and pepper**

For the court-bouillon:
- ○ **1 bouquet garni consisting of: 1 sprig thyme, 3 sprigs parsley, 2 bay leaves**
- ○ **1 clove garlic**
- ○ **2 small carrots, sliced**
- ○ **10 peppercorns**
- ○ **salt**

1. If you are using snails in their shells: cover the snails with 45ml (3 tbls) coarse salt and leave to soak for 2 hours. Wash well under running water.
2. To prepare the stock: in a large saucepan filled with water, place the bouquet garni, carrots, garlic, salt and peppercorns. Cook for 30 minutes. Add the snails, and cook for 1 hour over medium heat. If you are using tinned snails, cook them for only 10 minutes.
3. Preheat the oven to 200°C (400°F; gas mark 6).
4. Leave the snails to cool in the stock, then drain. If they are in their shells, remove them and wash and wipe the shells. Remove the black end of the snails, which is sometimes bitter. Put aside the snails and shells.
5. To prepare the stuffing: peel the garlic and chop finely. In a bowl, cream the butter, garlic and parsley. This should result in a very smooth paste. Season with salt and pepper to taste (use salt sparingly as the snails are salty).
6. Replace the snails in their shells, and fill the shells to the top with the garlic butter.
7. Place the snails in an ovenproof dish, with the holes upwards so that the butter does not leak out of the shells during cooking. Cook for 10 minutes, and serve at once.

Tomates au Basilic

Iced Tomato Soup with Basil

Serves 4. Preparation: 10 min Refrigeration: 30 min

★★

○ **8 red, ripe tomatoes**
○ **1 cucumber**
○ **4 sprigs fresh basil**
○ **juice of 1 lemon**
○ **celery salt**
○ **salt and pepper**

1. Bring some water to the boil. Wash the tomatoes, plunge them into the boiling water for 10 seconds, then peel and discard the seeds.
2. Peel the cucumber, remove the seeds with a sharp knife, and cut into pieces.
3. Place the cucumber and tomatoes in a liquidizer. Season with salt and pepper. Add the lemon juice. Blend for a few seconds.
4. Pour the mixture into a salad bowl or individual bowls, and leave to chill in the refrigerator for 30 minutes. Sprinkle with the chopped basil leaves before serving. Serve with celery salt.

Melon au Jambon et aux Figues

Melon with Parma Ham and Fresh Figs

Serves 4-8. Preparation: 10 min

★

○ **1 honeydew melon weighing 500g (18 oz)**
○ **8 very thin slices of Parma ham**
○ **8 fresh figs**
○ **pepper**

1. Cut the melon into 8 slices, scoop out the seeds and cut away the skin.
2. Tail and wash the figs. With a sharp knife, make 4 incisions lengthways in the skin of each fig, without cutting the flesh. Peel back the skin, leaving it attached to the fig, to form 4 petals.
3. Place the melon slices on a serving dish, alternating with the figs and ham. Pepper the melon generously.

Melon à l'Ananas et au Jambon

Melon with Pineapple and Smoked Ham

Serves 4. Preparation: 15 min
Refrigeration: 1 hr

★

○ **2 honeydew melons**
○ **1 thick slice smoked ham**
○ **1 pineapple slice**
○ **juice of 1 lemon**
○ **5ml (1 tsp) cognac**
○ **salt and pepper**

1. Halve the melons. Scoop out the seeds and flesh with a spoon. Keep the skins.
2. Dice the pineapple and melon.
3. In a bowl, carefully mix the lemon juice, diced pineapple and melon, and add the cognac. Season. Place in the refrigerator for 1 hour.
4. Before serving, dice the slice of ham and add to the melon mixture. Mix well. Fill the melon skins with the mixture. Serve at once.

You can vary this dish by filling the melon shells with diced cheese, ham and pickled onion or raisins.

Melon with port: Cut a hole in the end of a melon. Remove the seeds through the hole. Pour in 60ml (4 tbls) red port. Leave the melon in the refrigerator for at least 2 hours. Shake the melon from time to time so that the port moistens the flesh of the melon.

Melon mousse: In a liquidizer, blend the flesh of 1 melon with 45ml (3 tbls) double cream. Pour this mixture into individual bowls and refrigerate for 1 hour before serving.

Potage Glacé au Cresson
Iced Watercress Soup

Serves 4. Preparation: 15 min Cooking: 30 min
Refrigeration: 2 hr
★★

○ **1 bunch watercress**
○ **100ml (3½ fl oz) double cream**
○ **10 sprigs chervil, coarsely chopped (if available)**
○ **20g (¾ oz) butter**
○ **half a French stick**
○ **2 small cloves garlic**
○ **15ml (1 tbls) olive oil**
○ **salt and pepper**

1. Cut off and discard the stalks of the watercress, wash and drain the leaves. In a saucepan, melt the butter and cook the watercress for 10 minutes. Add 1 litre (approx 1¾ pints) hot water and cook uncovered for 20 minutes.
2. Meanwhile, peel and halve the garlic cloves; cut the bread lengthways and rub each cut side with the garlic. Cut the bread into small pieces (croûtons). Heat the oil in a frying pan over a medium heat. Cook the croûtons on both sides for 5 minutes until brown. Drain on absorbent paper.
3. When the soup is cooked, liquidize it and season. Add the cream and blend again. Pour the soup into a bowl and refrigerate for 2 hours.
4. Before serving, sprinkle with the chervil. Serve the garlic croûtons separately.

If you can't find fresh chervil, save a few leaves of watercress to garnish the soup.

Potage aux Concombres
Iced Cucumber Soup

Serves 4. Preparation and cooking: 25 min
Refrigeration: 2 hr
★★

○ **2 cucumbers**
○ **1 small clove garlic**
○ **1 red pepper**
○ **15ml (1 tbls) red wine vinegar**
○ **15ml (1 tbls) olive oil**
○ **10 sprigs parsley, coarsely chopped**
○ **salt and pepper**

1. Peel the cucumbers and cut into chunks, removing the seeds with a sharp knife. Peel and chop the garlic. Blend the cucumbers and garlic in a liquidizer.
2. Pour the purée into a hollow dish, add 1 litre (1¾ pints) water, a little at a time (if you prefer a thick soup, use less water). Add the vinegar and oil. Season highly with salt and pepper. Mix well and refrigerate for 2 hours.
3. Meanwhile, wash and dry the pepper. Grill on all sides, leave to cool, then peel. Remove the seeds and cut into thin strips.
4. Before serving, sprinkle the soup with the pepper strips and parsley.

Potage Glacé ' l'Oseille
Iced Sorrel Soup

Serves 4. Preparation: 10 min Cooking: 25 min
Refrigeration: 2 hr
★

○ **500g (18 oz) sorrel**
○ **100ml (3½ fl oz) double cream**
○ **20g (¾ oz) butter**
○ **10 fresh tarragon leaves**
○ **salt and pepper**

1. Discard the sorrel stalks; wash and drain the leaves. In a large saucepan, melt the butter over a low heat and add the sorrel. Cook for 5 minutes.
2. When the sorrel is soft, add 1 litre (1¾ pints) hot water. Season with salt and pepper. Cook, uncovered, over a high heat for 20 minutes.
3. Leave to cool, then add the cream. Mix with a whisk. Pour the soup into a bowl and refrigerate for 2 hours. Before serving, sprinkle with chopped tarragon.

Bouillon Glacé en Pastèque
Iced Consommé in Watermelon

Serves 4. Preparation: 20 min Cooking: 3 hr
Refrigeration: 1 hr
★★

○ **2 chicken legs**
○ **2 chicken wings**
○ **1 chicken neck**
○ **1 turnip**
○ **2 carrots**
○ **2 leeks**
○ **1 bouquet garni consisting of:**
   2 sprigs thyme, 2 sprigs
   parsley, 2 bay leaves
○ **1 clove garlic**
○ **2 egg whites, beaten**
○ **1 watermelon weighing 2kg**
   (4½ lb)
○ **150g (5 oz) chicken breast**
○ **1 green pepper**
○ **1 red pepper**
○ **12 button mushrooms**
○ **2 tomatoes**
○ **60ml (2 fl oz) sherry**
○ **5ml (1 tsp) peppercorns**
○ **2 pinches coarse salt**

1. Refrigerate the watermelon. Singe the wings and legs of the chicken over the flames of the cooker to remove any remaining feathers.
2. Peel the turnip and carrots, and prepare the leeks. Cut the carrots and leeks lengthways. Tie the leeks in a bunch with string. Peel the garlic.
3. In a large saucepan containing 2½ litres (4¼ pints) water, place the carrots, turnip, leeks, garlic, bouquet garni, peppercorns, chicken neck, wings, legs and breast.
4. Bring the stock to the boil, skim and reduce the heat. Simmer for 3 hours. Remove the chicken breast after 30 minutes and put aside.
5. After 3 hours, strain the stock and discard the flavouring ingredients. Replace over the heat, and add the egg whites, stirring all the time, to obtain a clear consommé. Cook over a low heat until it starts to 'shiver'. Remove from the heat and strain again. Leave to cool and refrigerate for 1 hour.
6. Bring some water to the boil and immerse the tomatoes for 10 seconds. Remove, peel, discard the seeds and chop the flesh. Wash the mushrooms and peppers. Seed and dice the peppers. Cut the mushrooms and chicken breast into thin strips.
7. Cut off the top of the watermelon. Remove the seeds and a little of the flesh. Pour the chicken stock into the melon and add the sherry. Garnish with the chicken and mushroom strips, diced peppers and chopped tomatoes.

Mulet aux Concombres
Mullet with Cucumbers

Serves 4. Preparation: 20 min Cooking: 15 min
Refrigeration: 1 hr
★★

○ **1 gray mullet weighing 1kg**
   (2¼ lb)
○ **2 cucumbers**
○ **juice of 1 lemon**
○ **90ml (6 tbls) mayonnaise**
○ **12 black olives**
○ **5 lettuce leaves**
○ **5ml (1 tsp) fennel seeds**
○ **salt and pepper**

1. Preheat the oven to 230°C (450°F; gas mark 8).
2. Clean, scale and wash the mullet. Keep it whole.
3. Scatter the fennel seeds inside the fish and place in an ovenproof dish. Season with salt and pepper. Pour into the dish 15ml (1 tbls) water, and cover with foil. Bake for 15 minutes.
4. Meanwhile, peel the cucumbers, remove the seeds with a sharp knife, and cut into slices. Place the slices in a bowl.
5. Stone the olives, and mince them as finely as possible. Add the lemon juice to the mayonnaise with the minced olives; season with pepper. Mix well. Pour the sauce over the cucumbers.
6. Remove the fish from the oven and discard the fennel seeds. Leave to cool, then refrigerate for 1 hour.
7. Place the lettuce leaves on a serving dish, top with the fish, and cover with the cucumber sauce.

You can also use red mullet or mackerel for this recipe, and chicory may replace the cucumbers.

Salade d'Avocats aux Oranges

Serves 4. Preparation: 20 min

Avocado and Orange Salad

★

- ○ **3 avocados**
- ○ **2 oranges**
- ○ **2 small onions (or pickling onions)**
- ○ **5ml (1 tsp) parsley, coarsely chopped**
- ○ **1 tomato**
- ○ **10 lettuce leaves**
- ○ **45ml (3 tbls) oil**
- ○ **15ml (1 tbls) vinegar**
- ○ **salt and pepper**

1. Halve 2 avocados, remove the stones and the skin with a sharp knife. Slice the flesh.
2. Peel and segment the oranges. Cut off the stalk end of the tomato, slice and discard the seeds. Peel the onions and slice, separating into rings.
3. Cut off the pointed end of the remaining avocado about one-third of the way down. Remove the stone. With a sharp knife, cut small v shapes around the top.
4. In a bowl, dissolve 3 pinches of salt in the vinegar, add the oil and season with pepper. Stir well.
5. Arrange the lettuce leaves in a serving dish, cover·with the sliced tomato, then alternate avocado slices and orange segments on top of the tomato. Garnish with the onion rings, sprinkle with parsley and place the third avocado in the centre of the dish. Pour the vinaigrette into the avocado 'bowl' and serve.

Caviar d'Aubergine

Serves 6. Preparation: 20 min Cooking: 20 min
Refrigeration: 2 hr

Aubergine Purée with Garlic

★★

- ○ **1.5kg (3¼ lb) aubergines**
- ○ **120ml (8 tbls) olive oil**
- ○ **1 bunch parsley, coarsely chopped**
- ○ **5 cloves garlic**
- ○ **salt and pepper**

1. Place the aubergines under a hot grill and cook, turning to cook all sides, about 20 minutes or until very soft.
2. Peel and finely chop the garlic.
3. When the aubergines have cooled, open them and scoop out the flesh. Place in a bowl and mash with a fork. Mix in the oil a little at a time, then add the garlic and parsley, and salt and pepper to taste. Mix well.
4. Refrigerate for 2 hours. Serve cold.

Fromage Blanc aux Herbes

Serves 6. Preparation: 10 min

Fromage Blanc with Herbs

★

- ○ **1 large carton fromage blanc or cream cheese**
- ○ **15ml (1 tbls) olive oil**
- ○ **1 bunch chervil, coarsely chopped**
- ○ **2 cloves garlic**
- ○ **salt and pepper**

1. Peel the garlic and chop finely.
2. In a bowl, mash the cheese with a fork, add the oil and garlic. Season with salt and generously with pepper. Mix carefully with a wooden spoon so that the oil and garlic blend well into the cheese. Finish off with a whisk. Add the chervil. Mix again and serve cold.

Serve this with toast. Instead of chervil, you can use chives, parsley, tarragon or fresh mint. If you use any of these herbs, do not add garlic. Refrigerate for at least 1 hour before serving.

Asperges en Salade
Asparagus Salad

Serves 4-8. Preparation: 15 min Cooking: 30 min

★★

○ **2kg (4½ lb) asparagus**
○ **2 tins asparagus tips weighing 200g (7 oz) each**
○ **90ml (6 tbls) mayonnaise made with lemon juice**
○ **coarse salt**

1. Add 15ml (1 tbls) of coarse salt to 1 litre (1¾ pints) water and bring to the boil.
2. Remove the base of the stems from the asparagus. Using a knife, scrape the white part of the stems downwards, to remove the hard skin. Wash well and tie them in a bundle.
3. Plunge the asparagus into the boiling water. Reduce heat, and simmer, uncovered, for 30 minutes.
4. Prepare some mayonnaise using the juice of half a lemon instead of vinegar.
5. Open the tins of asparagus, drain and rinse under running water.
6. In a liquidizer, purée the asparagus tips. Fold this into the mayonnaise and mix well.
7. Remove the asparagus from the water, drain and untie them. Serve the sauce separately.

Purée de Pois Chiches
Purée of Chick Peas

Serves 6. Preparation: 15 min

★

○ **1 tin (500g/18 oz) chick peas**
○ **120ml (8 tbls) olive oil**
○ **3 cloves garlic**
○ **5 sprigs parsley, coarsely chopped**
○ **1 lemon**
○ **salt**

1. In a large saucepan, bring some salted water to the boil. Open the tin of chick peas and drain. Plunge the chick peas into the water, cook for 2 minutes and drain.
2. Peel and crush the garlic. Mash the chick peas with a fork or purée them in a liquidizer. Place them in a bowl and add the olive oil, a little at a time, using a whisk. Add the garlic, mix well and leave to cool.
3. Before serving, sprinkle with the parsley and garnish with lemon wedges.

This purée is delicious spread on toast.

Salade d'Oronges aux Fruits
Mushroom Salad with Fruit

Serves 4. Preparation: 20 min

★

○ **400g (14 oz) mushrooms**
○ **100g (4 oz) Tomme de Savoie cheese (or substitute any mild, medium-soft cheese)**
○ **1 tart apple**
○ **1 orange**
○ **60ml (4 tbls) oil**
○ **juice of 1 lemon**
○ **salt and pepper**
○ **1 small celeriac**

1. Trim the earthy base off the mushroom stalks, and wash them under running water. Wash and peel the celeriac. Peel the apple and remove the core. Cut the mushrooms, celeriac and apple into julienne strips. Place them in a salad bowl and sprinkle with a little of the lemon juice.
2. Remove the crust from the cheese, and dice. Peel the orange and remove the white skin from the segments. Chop the flesh finely. Add to the ingredients in the bowl.
3. In a small bowl, dissolve a few pinches of salt in the remaining lemon juice, add the oil and season with pepper. Mix well. Pour this sauce over the salad and serve at once.

As a cold hors d'oeuvre, you can serve vegetables cut into strips or small pieces, to be dipped into a variety of sauces: mustard, anchovy and tartare, for example.

Salade de Cervelle et de Laitue

Serves 4. Preparation: 15 min Cooking: 5 min

Brain and Lettuce Salad

★ ★

- ○ **1 calf's brain**
- ○ **1 lettuce**
- ○ **1 cucumber**
- ○ **75ml (5 tbls) mustardy mayonnaise**
- ○ **100g (4 oz) button mushrooms**
- ○ **150g (6 oz) prawns**
- ○ **1 small onion**
- ○ **3 sprigs parsley**
- ○ **15ml (1 tbls) wine vinegar**
- ○ **10 sprigs chervil, coarsely chopped**
- ○ **5ml (1 tsp) capers**
- ○ **juice of ½ lemon**
- ○ **salt and pepper**

1. Peel the onion and wash the parsley. Fill a saucepan with water, add the vinegar and a pinch of salt, then add onion and parsley. Bring to the boil, add the calf's brain and poach for 5 minutes. Drain and put aside.
2. Wash the lettuce and shake off excess water. Peel the cucumber, remove the seeds with a sharp knife, and cut into thin slices. Trim the earthy base off the mushrooms, wash and cut into thin strips. Shell the prawns. Mix all the ingredients in a salad bowl.
3. Prepare a mayonnaise with extra mustard. To 75ml (5 tbls), add the capers, lemon juice and pepper. Fold the mayonnaise into the salad.
4. Snip away the fibres of the brain, and cut into slices. Place them in the salad bowl. Do not mix. Sprinkle with chervil and serve at once.

Champignons à la Grecque

Serves 4. Preparation: 15 min Cooking: 20 min

Mushrooms à la Grecque

 ★ ★

- ○ **500g (18 oz) button mushrooms**
- ○ **120ml (4 fl oz) white wine**
- ○ **30ml (2 tbls) olive oil**
- ○ **3 tomatoes**
- ○ **1 small onion**
- ○ **10 coriander seeds**
- ○ **1 bouquet garni consisting of: 2 sprigs thyme, 2 bay leaves**
- ○ **juice of 1 lemon**
- ○ **salt and pepper**

1. Trim off the earthy base of the mushrooms and wash. Keep them whole.
2. In a large saucepan, bring some water to the boil. Plunge the tomatoes in the water for 10 seconds. Drain, peel, remove the seeds, then mash with a fork.
3. Peel the onion and slice thinly. Put the oil into a saucepan over a low heat. Add the onion, mushrooms, tomatoes, bouquet garni, wine and coriander seeds. Season with salt and pepper. Simmer, uncovered, for 20 minutes.
4. Pour the ingredients into a salad bowl, having removed the bouquet garni. Squeeze the lemon juice over the salad. Serve cold.

For this recipe, you can use small onions or small artichokes instead of mushrooms. If you use artichokes, cut them in half before cooking.

Carottes Piquantes

Serves 4. Preparation: 10 min Cooking: 25 min

Spicy Carrots

★

- ○ **1kg (2¼ lb) carrots**
- ○ **5ml (1 tsp) cumin**
- ○ **5ml (1 tsp) harissa or hot chilli sauce**
- ○ **4 cloves garlic**
- ○ **1 small onion**
- ○ **60ml (4 tbls) oil**
- ○ **salt and pepper**

1. Scrape, peel and slice the carrots. Peel the garlic and onion, and chop finely.
2. Pour the oil into a saucepan, add the carrots, garlic, onion and harissa. Season with salt and pepper. Cover with water and bring to the boil. Then add the cumin, reduce the heat and cook until the water has evaporated. Remove from the heat and allow to cool.

You can apply this recipe to other vegetables such as leeks, onions and small turnips.

Fenouils en Marinade

Serves 4. Preparation: 15 min Marinade: 24 hr

Marinated Fennel

★

○ **2 heads fennel**

For the marinade:
○ **2 lemons**
○ **45ml (3 tbls) olive oil**
○ **15ml (1 tbls) wine vinegar**
○ **15ml (1 tbls) capers**
○ **3 sprigs tarragon**
○ **salt and pepper**

1. Trim off the bases and stems of the fennel. Wash, halve them and cut into strips. Place in a shallow dish.
2. Prepare the marinade: peel and slice the lemons. Remove the stalks of the tarragon. In a bowl, place the oil, vinegar, capers, tarragon leaves, salt and pepper. Add the slices of lemon and mix.
3. Pour the marinade over the fennel and refrigerate for 24 hours. Drain and serve.

Other vegetables, such as onions, diced carrots, white or red cabbage, peppers, cucumbers, black radishes or celery, can be marinated in the same way. This marinade may also be used for poached fish: cod, anglerfish, tuna.

Try serving an assortment of marinated vegetables, accompanied by gherkins, olives and marinated mozzarella cheese, which you prepare in the following way: cover slices of cheese with olive oil, garnish each slice with an anchovy and sprinkle with oregano or thyme.

Salade de Foies et de Pommes de Terre

Serves 4-6. Preparation: 20 min Cooking: 20 min

Chicken Liver and Potato Salad

★★

○ **10 potatoes**
○ **3 eggs**
○ **300g (10 oz) chicken liver**
○ **50g (2 oz) tin anchovies in oil**
○ **30ml (2 tbls) olive oil**
○ **juice of 1½ lemons**
○ **30g (1¼ oz) butter**
○ **5ml (1 tsp) parsley, coarsely chopped**
○ **salt and pepper**

1. Wash the potatoes. Cook them in their jackets for 20 minutes in boiling salted water. Meanwhile, hard boil the eggs.
2. Cut the chicken livers into pieces. Melt the butter in a frying pan and fry the livers for a few minutes, until they become tender. Put aside. Open the tin of anchovies. Pour away the oil and fry the anchovies in a small saucepan, until they become a paste.
3. Remove the eggs from the water and drain the potatoes.
4. In a large bowl, dissolve a pinch of salt in the lemon juice. Add the anchovy paste and olive oil. Season with pepper.
5. Skin the potatoes while still warm. Slice them and place in the salad bowl. Mix with the sauce. Add the chicken livers. Mix again. Top the salad with the sliced hard-boiled eggs and sprinkle with parsley. Serve still warm.

Choose boiling potatoes which will not flake after cooking. The potatoes must still be warm when dressed with the sauce, so that they will absorb it properly.

Why not excite your guests' appetite with something different? Try serving raw vegetables à la croque au sel *(with buttered bread and salt). Serve broad beans, small green peppers or small artichokes.*

Cocktail Marin

Seafood Cocktail

Serves 4. Preparation and cooking: 50 min
Refrigeration: 2 hr
★★

○ **500g (18 oz) mussels**
○ **500g (18 oz) cockles**
○ **200g (7 oz) small cuttlefish**
○ **200g (7 oz) octopus**
○ **200g (7 oz) prawns**
○ **2 red peppers**
○ **150g (5 oz) green and black olives**
○ **30g (1¼ oz) small gherkins**
○ **2 cloves garlic**
○ **15ml (1 tbls) vinegar**
○ **100ml (3½ fl oz) oil**
○ **juice of 1 lemon**
○ **1 bunch parsley**
○ **salt and pepper**

1. Wash and dry the peppers. Grill them on all sides for about 15 minutes or until the skin turns black and becomes shrivelled. Leave to cool.
2. Scrub the mussels well, scrape away their beards, wash well under running water and drain. Wash the cockles in water with a little vinegar added, rubbing them between your hands. Rinse well and drain.
3. Place the mussels and cockles in a large saucepan with 1½cm (½ in) water, and cook, uncovered, over a high heat until they open. Drain and remove them from their shells. Put aside.
4. Clean the octopus and cuttlefish by removing their ink sacs, mouths, eyes and inner bones. Skin and wash repeatedly under cold running water. Cook in boiling salted water for 10 minutes. Drain and put aside.
5. Shell the prawns.
6. Roughly chop the octopus, and place in a large bowl with the whole cuttlefish, prawns, mussels and cockles.
7. Remove the skin and seeds from the peppers with a sharp knife. Cut into thin strips. Stone and halve the olives. Cut the gherkins into small pieces. Place all the ingredients in the bowl.
8. To prepare the sauce: peel the garlic and crush it into a bowl. Dissolve the salt in the lemon juice and add, along with the oil; season with pepper. Pour the sauce over the salad, mix carefully and refrigerate for 2 hours. Just before serving, wash the parsley, remove the stalks, chop and garnish the salad with the leaves.

Crevettes et Crabe en Pamplemousse

Shrimp and Crab Cocktail in Grapefruit

Serves 4. Preparation: 20 min
★★

○ **2 large grapefruit**
○ **200g (7 oz) shrimps**
○ **1 tin (200g/7 oz) crabmeat**
○ **1 small mango**

For the sauce:
○ **60ml (4 tbls) mayonnaise**
○ **15ml (1 tbls) cognac**
○ **200ml (7 fl oz) double cream**
○ **1 pinch cayenne pepper**

1. Halve the grapefruit. Gently scoop out the flesh with a teaspoon and dice. Place in a salad bowl. Reserve the skins.
2. Shell the shrimps. Open the tin of crabmeat, rinse under running water, and drain. Flake the crabmeat, removing any cartilage which might have been left in. Add to the diced grapefruit.
3. Peel the mango and dice the flesh, discarding the stone. Add the mango to the bowl.
4. In a small bowl, beat the cream lightly with a whisk and fold into the mayonnaise with the cognac and cayenne pepper. Blend well.
5. Pour the sauce over the salad and mix gently. Fill the grapefruit skins with the salad and serve.

Shellfish do not take long to cook when grilled or cooked over a high heat.

Shellfish such as clams or mussels should open after cooking for a short time. If they remain closed, this indicates that they are no longer fresh and should be discarded.

Salade de Crevettes aux Fruits
Shrimp and Fruit Salad

Serves 4. Preparation: 15 min

★

○ **250g (9 oz) prawns**
○ **1 small mango**
○ **2 bananas**
○ **juice of 1 lemon**
○ **60ml (4 tbls) mayonnaise**
○ **45ml (3 tbls) double cream**
○ **5ml (1 tsp) mango chutney**
○ **1 pinch sugar**
○ **15ml (1 tbls) cognac**
○ **1 drop Tabasco sauce**
○ **10 lettuce leaves**

1. Shell the prawns and place them in a salad bowl. Peel and dice the mango and add to the prawns. Peel and slice the bananas and sprinkle with the lemon juice to prevent discoloration.
2. Add to the mayonnaise the mango chutney, sugar, cognac and Tabasco. Whisk the cream lightly and add. Blend all the ingredients well.
3. Mix the sauce gently into the fruit and prawns.
4. Place the lettuce leaves in a dish, and top with the salad mixture. Refrigerate until ready to serve.

Salade de Saumon et de Gambas
Salmon and Giant Prawn Salad

Serves 4. Preparation and cooking: 20 min

★★

○ **150g (5 oz) giant prawns**
○ **2 slices smoked salmon**
○ **1 tin (200g/7 oz) crabmeat**
○ **1 tin (50g/2 oz) anchovies in oil**
○ **1 red pepper**

For the sauce:
○ **100ml (3½ fl oz) oil**
○ **100ml (3½ fl oz) double cream**
○ **juice of 1 lemon**
○ **1 pinch paprika**
○ **salt and pepper**

1. Drain the crabmeat, removing any cartilage which might have been left in. Flake and place in a salad bowl. Drain off the oil from the anchovies and add them to the crab.
2. Cut the salmon into small pieces. Cut the pepper into strips. Put aside.
3. Grill the prawns for 2 minutes on each side. Leave to cool slightly.
4. In a liquidizer, place the salmon, lemon juice, cream, oil and salt and pepper. Blend until you obtain a smooth sauce. Add to the salad mixture. Sprinkle with paprika.
5. Shell the prawns while still warm and add them to the salad. Gently mix all the ingredients together. Garnish with pepper strips. Serve at once.

Salade de Moules et Pommes de Terre
Mussel and Potato Salad

Serves 4-6. Preparation: 20 min Cooking: 30 min

★★

○ **1kg (2¼ lb) potatoes**
○ **3 litres (approx 6½ lb) mussels**
○ **200ml (7 fl oz) double cream**
○ **1 onion**
○ **juice of 1 lemon**
○ **1 bouquet garni consisting of: 1 sprig thyme, 2 bay leaves, 3 sprigs parsley**
○ **60ml (4 tbls) olive oil**
○ **5 finely chopped gherkins**
○ **5 chive leaves, coarsely chopped**
○ **5 sprigs chervil, coarsely chopped**
○ **240ml (9 fl oz) white wine**
○ **salt and pepper**

1. Scrub the mussels, scrape away their beards, and wash well under running water. Place in a saucepan over a high heat, with the onion and bouquet garni. Shake from time to time, and remove from the heat when the mussels have opened. Drain and remove the shells. Put aside.
2. Cook the potatoes, in their jackets, in boiling salted water for 20 to 25 minutes. Peel and slice them while still hot, and pour the wine over them.
3. To prepare the sauce: in a bowl, dissolve the salt in the lemon juice and add the cream. Stir in the oil, add the herbs and chopped gherkins. Season with pepper. Mix well.
4. In a salad bowl, place alternate layers of potatoes, mussels and sauce.

Moules à l'Ailloli
Mussels in Aioli

Serves 4. Preparation: 20 min Cooking: 10 min

★★

○ **2 litres (4½ lb) mussels**

For the aioli:
○ **3 cloves garlic**
○ **1 egg yolk**
○ **juice of 1 lemon**
○ **240ml (9 fl oz) olive oil**
○ **salt and pepper**

1. Scrub the mussels, scrape away their beards, and wash well under running water. Place in a saucepan, uncovered, over a high heat, shaking from time to time. Remove from the heat when they have opened. Drain.
2. To prepare the aioli: peel and crush the garlic. Place the egg yolk and garlic in a bowl; stir well and leave to stand for 1 hour. Then, stirring all the time with a wooden spoon, add the oil a little at a time, as if you were making mayonnaise. Finish with a whisk. The aioli must be almost solid. Add the lemon juice and salt and pepper.
3. Remove the mussels from their shells. In a shallow dish, mix the mussels and aioli. Serve at once.

You can serve this dish with hot croûtons. It is also good with finely chopped herbs added to the aioli.

Salade de Poulpe
Octopus Salad

Serves 4. Preparation: 15 min Cooking: 1 hr

★★

○ **1 octopus weighing approx 1kg (2¼ lb)**
○ **4 cloves garlic**
○ **45ml (3 tbls) olive oil**
○ **juice of 1 lemon**
○ **5 sprigs fresh basil, coarsely chopped**
○ **pepper**

1. Clean the octopus, remove its ink sac and rinse well under running water. Place in a saucepan and cook, without water, over a low heat until red and tender. Drain, cut into small pieces and place in a salad bowl.
2. Peel and crush the garlic. In a small bowl, mix the garlic, lemon juice and oil. Season with pepper. Pour the sauce over the chopped octopus, and leave in the refrigerator for ½ hour. Before serving, sprinkle with chopped fresh basil leaves.

You can garnish this dish with sliced tomatoes and lemon wedges.

Cocktail de Crabe
Crab Cocktail

Serves 4. Preparation: 15 min Cooking: 10 min

★

○ **1 tin (200g/7 oz) crabmeat**
○ **4 eggs**
○ **90ml (6 tbls) mayonnaise**
○ **15ml (1 tbls) tomato purée or ketchup**
○ **salt and pepper**

1. Place the eggs in a small saucepan, cover with cold water and cook for 10 minutes.
2. Add tomato purée or ketchup to the mayonnaise, mix well. Season with salt and pepper to taste.
3. Drain the crabmeat, removing any cartilage which might have been left in. Flake the crab.
4. Drain the eggs, cool under running water, shell and dice them.
5. In a bowl, mix the crab with the mayonnaise. Add the diced eggs, mixing gently. Turn the salad into individual bowls. Serve cold.

The aioli from Marseilles is a complete dish in itself. Pound some garlic in a mortar, and bind it with some bread (crusts removed) and an egg yolk. Then add olive oil, a little at a time. Aioli is served with vegetables, poached cod or snails. In Provence, one binds the garlic with the egg yolk only – no bread is used – and it is served as it is, or mixed with saffron and served with shellfish.

Tarama
Taramasalata

Serves 4. Preparation: 10 min

★

○ **200g (7 oz) smoked cod's roe**
○ **juice of 1 lemon**
○ **1 slice white bread**
○ **30ml (2 tbls) milk**
○ **30ml (2 tbls) oil**
○ **12 black olives**

1. Bring some water to the boil in a saucepan. Place the cod's roe in the boiling water for a few seconds. Drain and remove the skin.
2. Soak the bread in the milk. In a bowl, mash the roe with the bread. Add the lemon juice and stir with a fork, adding the oil a little at a time. Serve with black olives.

You can use a vegetable mill for this recipe. The bread and milk can be replaced with 45ml (3 tbls) double cream.

Salade de Crustacés
Shellfish Salad

Serves 4. Preparation: 30 min

★ ★

○ **1 tin (200g/7 oz) crabmeat**
○ **150g (5 oz) prawns**
○ **1 litre (2½ lb) cockles**
○ **12 oysters**
○ **1 tin (50g/2 oz) anchovy fillets in oil**
○ **30ml (2 tbls) capers**
○ **30ml (2 tbls) French mustard**
○ **45ml (3 tbls) oil**
○ **juice of 1 lemon**
○ **1 bunch watercress**
○ **5ml (1 tsp) chervil, coarsely chopped**
○ **salt and pepper**

1. Wash the cockles. Cook over a high heat until they open. Drain and remove from their shells.
2. Open the oysters. Pour their juice into a saucepan, and bring to the boil. Poach the oysters in this juice for 1 minute and drain.
3. Drain the crabmeat and anchovy fillets. Remove any cartilage from the crabmeat. Shell the prawns. Cut off the stalks of the watercress, wash the leaves and drain.
4. Place the mustard in a bowl, and add the oil a little at a time, stirring continuously. Season, with salt and pepper, and add the capers, lemon juice and chervil. Mix all ingredients well.
5. In a bowl, mix together the watercress, oysters, cockles and sauce; place the crabmeat in the centre, surrounded with prawns and anchovy fillets. Serve.

Salade de Maquereaux
Mackerel Salad

Serves 4. Preparation: 20 min Cooking: 20 min

★

○ **2 mackerel**
○ **4 potatoes**
○ **15ml (1 tbls) vinegar**
○ **30ml (2 tbls) oil**
○ **4 chives, finely chopped**
○ **60ml (2 fl oz) white wine**
○ **salt and pepper**

1. Cook the potatoes in salted water for 20 minutes. Bring some water to the boil in another saucepan. Clean the mackerel and cut off their heads. Poach in boiling water for 10 minutes. Drain and remove the bones and skin. Cut the flesh into pieces.
2. Place the pieces of mackerel in a salad bowl and pour over the wine, then add the vinegar and oil. Season with salt and pepper. Add the chives. Peel and slice the potatoes while still warm, and add to the salad. Mix well and serve at once.

Fish can be the basis of a good sauce. A few examples: anchovy fillets and garlic which you pound together and to which you add some olive oil; purée of smoked herring to which you add some oil, lemon juice and herbs; fish leftovers (such as tuna or cod) reduced to a purée with onion and tarragon leaves. You can also mix these leftovers with lemon butter and parsley.

These sauces may be served with poached or grilled fish. They are also delicious with potato, tomato or other salads.

Acras de Morue

Serves 6. Preparation: 20 min Cooking: 20 min

Cod Croquettes

★★

○ **400g (14 oz) salt cod fillets**
○ **2 cloves garlic**
○ **1 bunch parsley, coarsely chopped**
○ **10ml (2 tsp) paprika, mild or hot**
○ **30g (1¼ oz) breadcrumbs**
○ **30g (1¼ oz) flour**
○ **1 egg**
○ **240ml (9 fl oz) oil**

1. Soak the cod fillets in water overnight. Drain and rinse thoroughly under running water.
2. Bring some water to the boil. Poach the cod in boiling water for 5 minutes. Drain and remove bones and skin. Flake the fish as finely as possible.
3. Peel the garlic and chop finely. Mix the flour with half a glass of water, and whisk in the egg. In a bowl, mix this sauce with the fish, add the paprika and the parsley. Mix well.
4. Form the mixture into small balls. Place the breadcrumbs on a plate and roll the fish balls in them.
5. Heat the oil in a frying pan. Fry the fish balls in hot oil for 2 minutes on each side, or until brown.

Acras are a delicious West Indian speciality. You can serve them with a sauce of pepper, lemon mayonnaise and half an avocado, reduced to a smooth paste in a liquidizer.

Harengs Fumés aux Poireaux

Serves 4. Preparation: 10 min Cooking: 20 min Marinade: 48 hr

Smoked Herrings with Leeks

★

○ **400g (14 oz) smoked herrings**
○ **250g (9 oz) carrots**
○ **2 large onions**
○ **1 sprig thyme**
○ **½ litre (18 fl oz) oil**
○ **2 bay leaves**
○ **cloves**
○ **1kg (2¼ lb) leeks**
○ **1 lemon**
○ **salt and pepper**

1. Prepare a marinade for the herrings: peel the carrots and cut into thin slices. Peel and slice the onions. In a deep dish, place a layer of herrings, some carrots and then some onions and 3 cloves. Repeat until there are no ingredients left. Add the oil, and make sure it runs to the bottom of the dish. Add the bay leaves and thyme. Marinate for 48 hours at the bottom of the refrigerator.
2. Trim and wash the leeks. Tie the white parts in a bundle and cook in salted water for 20 minutes (or for 10 minutes in a pressure cooker).
3. Meanwhile, drain the herrings and some of the carrots and onions. Serve 1 or 2 herrings per person. Place them on a serving dish, garnish with carrots and onions and surround with the drained but still warm leeks. Season with salt and pepper. Serve with lemon wedges.

Fish can be eaten raw: large sardines, for example. Remove the scales and head, cut them in half and discard the backbone, then cut the flesh into thin strips. Marinate with olive oil, lemon slices, pepper and thyme for 4 hours in the refrigerator. Drain and eat them with bread and butter: they are delicious. You can also prepare a variety of fish fillets in the same way. The marinade can be altered slightly, for example: oil, ground ginger and pepper, or oil, white wine, green pepper and onions.

Pain de Thon au Persil

Tuna Loaf with Parsley

Serves 4-6. Preparation: 20 min
Refrigeration: 2 hr
★★

○ **2 tins tuna weighing 400g (14 oz) each**
○ **4g (¼ oz) unflavoured, powdered gelatine**
○ **45ml (3 tbls) mayonnaise**
○ **1 bunch parsley**
○ **15ml (1 tbls) capers**
○ **12 gherkins**
○ **10g (½ oz) butter**
○ **6 lettuce leaves**
○ **10 small pickled onions**

1. Wash and dry the parsley. Finely chop 8 of the gherkins, the capers and parsley.
2. Drain the tuna and flake with a fork.
3. Dissolve the gelatine in a few spoonfuls of warm water.
4. In a large bowl, mix the parsley, gherkins, capers, tuna, mayonnaise and gelatine.
5. Butter a soufflé dish or mould and fill it with the tuna mixture. Refrigerate for 2 hours.
6. To unmould, place the dish or mould in hot water for a few seconds, and turn out onto a plate covered with lettuce leaves. Garnish with 4 gherkins and the pickled onions.

Pain de Cabillaud

Cod Loaf

Serves 4. Preparation: 15 min Cooking: 40 min
★★

○ **500g (18 oz) cooked cod**
○ **4 large potatoes**
○ **2 eggs**
○ **5 tomatoes**
○ **15ml (1 tbls) olive oil**
○ **30g (1¼ oz) butter**
○ **1 clove garlic, finely chopped**
○ **15ml (1 tbls) double cream**
○ **salt and pepper**

1. Preheat the oven to 200°C (400°F; gas mark 6).
2. Bring some water to the boil. Plunge the tomatoes in the water for 10 seconds. Peel them and remove the seeds. Heat the oil in a frying pan over a low heat, add the tomatoes and mash with a fork. Season and simmer for about 20 minutes.
3. Peel the potatoes and cook them in salted water for 20 minutes. Flake the fish into a bowl, add the potatoes and mash together with a fork. Add the beaten eggs and fold in the cream. Season to taste.
4. Butter a deep ovenproof dish. Pour in the ingredients and bake for 20 minutes. Add the garlic to the tomato sauce and serve it with the cod loaf.

Sardines Farcies

Stuffed Sardines

Serves 6. Preparation: 20 min Cooking: 15 min
★★★

○ **1kg (2¼ lb) medium-sized sardines**
○ **4 onions**
○ **4 shallots**
○ **4 cloves garlic**
○ **half a French stick**
○ **cayenne pepper**
○ **1 egg yolk**
○ **50g (2 oz) flour**
○ **1 bunch parsley, stalks removed**
○ **240ml (9 fl oz) oil**
○ **240ml (9 fl oz) milk**
○ **salt and pepper**

1. Cut off the heads of the sardines, clean and scrape them. With a sharp knife, cut the bellies lengthways and pull out the backbones. Leave them opened.
2. To prepare the stuffing: discard the crust of the bread, crumb the inside and soak in the milk. Peel the onions, shallots and garlic, chop finely and place in a bowl. Add the parsley; drain the bread and add to the ingredients in the bowl. Mix well, season with salt and pepper and 1 or 2 pinches of cayenne pepper, according to taste. Bind with the egg yolk.
3. Place the flour on a plate. Fill the sardines with the stuffing, close up and roll them in the flour.
4. Heat the oil in a frying pan. Fry the sardines for 2 minutes on each side in the hot oil and serve at once.

Coquilles Saint-Jacques à la Portugaise
Scallops Portuguese Style

Serves 4. Preparation: 20 min
Cooking: 45 min
★★★

- ○ **8 scallops**
- ○ **2 carrots**
- ○ **1 onion**
- ○ **1 bouquet garni consisting of:**
  1 sprig thyme, 2 bay leaves, 3
  sprigs parsley
- ○ **4 cloves**
- ○ **200ml (7 fl oz) white wine**
- ○ **100g (4 oz) butter**
- ○ **4 large tomatoes**
- ○ **100g (4 oz) button mushrooms**
- ○ **juice of half a lemon**
- ○ **50g (2 oz) grated Parmesan**
  cheese
- ○ **coarse salt, peppercorns**
- ○ **salt and pepper**

1. Place the scallops under the grill until they open. Cut through and remove the hinge muscle with a sharp knife, and detach the shells. Scrape off the beard-like fringe and the black intestinal thread. Keep the white flesh with the coral attached. Rinse well under running water. Put aside 4 shells.
2. Prepare a court-boullion: peel the carrots and cut in half lengthways. Peel the onion, and stick 4 cloves into it. Put 10ml (2 tsp) coarse salt into a large saucepan filled with water, add the carrots, onion, bouquet garni, 5 ml (1 tsp) peppercorns and the white wine. Simmer for 20 minutes. Strain the stock through a sieve. Bring back to the boil, then plunge the scallops into it and poach for 2 minutes. Remove from heat and drain.
3. Preheat the oven to 200°C (400°F; gas mark 6).
4. In another saucepan, bring some water to the boil. Plunge the tomatoes into the boiling water for 10 seconds. Drain, peel and remove the seeds. Remove the earthy base of the stem from the mushrooms, wash and cut them into strips.
5. Melt the butter in a flameproof casserole, add the tomatoes and mash with a fork, then add the mushrooms and lemon juice. Cook, uncovered, for 10 minutes. Season. Add the white flesh and coral of the scallops. Cook for a further 2 minutes over a low heat.
6. Spoon the mixture into the shells, sprinkle with Parmesan and place in the oven. Cook for 10 minutes, or until lightly browned. Serve at once.

Coquilles Saint-Jacques Gratinées
Scallops in Cream Sauce

Serves 4. Preparation: 15 min
Cooking: 35 min
★★

- ○ **8 scallops**
- ○ **150g (5 oz) button mushrooms**
- ○ **200ml (7 fl oz) double cream**
- ○ **3 shallots**
- ○ **60ml (2 fl oz) white wine**
- ○ **60g (2¼ oz) butter**
- ○ **20g (¾ oz) breadcrumbs**
- ○ **salt and pepper**

1. Place the scallops under a hot grill until they open. Detach the shells with a sharp knife. Keep 4 shells and clean them. Rinse the white flesh and the coral, cut the white part into large pieces.
2. Preheat the oven to 200°C (400°F; gas mark 6).
3. Peel the shallots, chop finely. Remove the earthy base of the stem from the mushrooms, wash and chop them finely. In 50g (2 oz) butter, brown the shallots, mushrooms, white flesh and coral of the scallops. Stir for 5 minutes, then add the white wine. Season. Cook for 10 minutes, then reduce the heat. Add the cream and cook for a further 10 minutes, but do not allow to boil.
4. Fill the shells with the mixture, sprinkle with breadcrumbs and with knobs of the remaining butter. Bake for 10 minutes, until lightly brown.

The best time for enjoying shellfish is during the autumn and winter months. Shellfish can be cooked in various ways, but some of them have a delicate flavour and are delicious eaten raw, with a squeeze of lemon.

Coquilles Saint-Jacques à la Ciboulette
Scallops with Chives

Serves 6. Preparation: 20 min
Marinade: 30 min
★

○ **18 scallops**
○ **juice of 4 lemons**
○ **1 bunch chives**
○ **100ml (3½ fl oz) olive oil**
○ **100ml (3½ fl oz) groundnut oil**
○ **5 shallots**
○ **45ml (3 tbls) chopped green pepper**

1. Place the scallops under a grill until they open. Detach the shells with a sharp knife and keep 6. Remove the beard-like fringe and black intestinal thread. Keep only the white flesh with the coral. Rinse well and cut into pieces.
2. Peel and chop the shallots. Wash the chives and chop them roughly.
3. Place the flesh of the scallops in a dish. Add the 2 kinds of oil, lemon juice, shallots, green pepper and chives. Mix well and marinate for 30 minutes in the refrigerator.
4. Fill the shells with the strained scallop mixture, and pour over each shell a little of the marinade. Serve the rest of the marinade separately in a sauceboat. Accompany with lemon quarters.

Coquilles Saint-Jacques aux Poireaux
Scallops with Leeks

Serves 6. Preparation: 20 min
Cooking: 35 min
★★

○ **18 scallops**
○ **1.5kg (3¼ lb) leeks**
○ **400ml (14 fl oz) double cream**
○ **25g (1 oz) butter**
○ **1 pinch grated nutmeg**
○ **1 pinch cayenne pepper**
○ **salt and pepper**

1. Place the scallops under the grill until they open. Detach the shells with a sharp knife and discard. Remove the beard-like fringe and the intestinal black thread. Keep only the white flesh and coral. Rinse under running water.
2. Preheat the oven to 200°C (400°F; gas mark 6).
3. Clean the leeks, keeping only the white part. Tie them in a bundle and cook in salted boiling water for 20 minutes. When they are tender, remove and rinse in cold water, then drain by pressing carefully in your hands.
4. Butter an ovenproof dish, make a nest of the leeks and top with the scallops. Season with salt and pepper and a pinch of cayenne pepper. Pour over the cream, and sprinkle with grated nutmeg.
5. Bake for 10 to 15 minutes.

Vénus Sauce Moutarde
Clams in Mustard Sauce

Serves 4. Preparation: 10 min Cooking: 10 min
★

○ **1kg (2¼ lb) clams**
○ **200ml (7 fl oz) double cream**
○ **15ml (1 tbls) French mustard**
○ **1 bunch parsley, roughly chopped**
○ **15ml (1 tbls) vinegar**
○ **salt and pepper**

1. Scrub the clams in water and a little vinegar, rubbing between your hands to remove any grit. Rinse well in cold water and drain.
2. Place them in a saucepan over a medium heat until they open, shaking from time to time.
3. Meanwhile, prepare the sauce: in a bowl, mix the cream and mustard, add the parsley, season with salt and pepper. This will result in a light yellow paste. Remove the clams from the heat, keeping some of their juice to add to the sauce. Place the clams in a dish and cover with the sauce. Mix well and serve warm.

Huîtres Gratinées

Serves 4. Preparation: 20 min Cooking: 10 min

Oysters au Gratin

★★

- ○ 18 oysters
- ○ 1 small clove garlic
- ○ 100g (4 oz) softened butter
- ○ 10 sprigs parsley, roughly chopped
- ○ juice of half a lemon
- ○ 20g (¾ oz) breadcrumbs
- ○ pepper

1. Preheat the oven to 250°C (475°F; gas mark 9).
2. Open the oysters, but leave them in their shells. Drain off their juice and set aside. Peel and crush the garlic.
3. In a bowl, place the softened butter, lemon juice, garlic, chopped parsley and a little of the juice from the oysters. Season with pepper. Mix well.
4. Place a little of this mixture on top of each oyster. Sprinkle with breadcrumbs and cook in the oven for 10 minutes, until brown.

Coques aux Echalotes

Serves 4. Preparation: 10 min Cooking: 15 min

Cockles with Shallots

★★

- ○ 3 litres (6½ lb) cockles
- ○ 6 shallots
- ○ 50ml (3 large tbls) double cream
- ○ 45ml (3 tbls) wine vinegar
- ○ 10 sprigs parsley, roughly chopped
- ○ 10g (½ oz) butter
- ○ pepper

1. Wash the cockles in water mixed with 30ml (2 tbls) vinegar, then rinse in water, rubbing them together in your hands. Drain.
2. Peel the shallots and chop roughly. Melt the butter in a saucepan and gently fry the shallots, moistening with a little hot water. Cook over a low heat for 10 minutes.
3. Meanwhile, place the cockles in a saucepan over a high heat for approximately 10 minutes until they open, shaking the pan from time to time. Remove from heat. Keep 45ml (3 tbls) of the juice.
4. Add 15ml (1 tbls) vinegar to the shallots. Cook for 1 minute, add the cream, season with pepper, and leave the sauce to boil for a few minutes, then add the cockle juice. Mix well and remove from the heat.
5. Place the cockles in a dish, pour the sauce over them and sprinkle with parsley. Serve at once.

Gratin de Fruits de Mer

Serves 4. Preparation: 30 min Cooking: 45 min

Shellfish au Gratin

★★

- ○ 200g (7 oz) cod fillets
- ○ 1kg (2¼ lb) mussels
- ○ 150g (5 oz) prawns
- ○ 1kg (2¼ lb) fresh spinach
- ○ 50g (2 oz) Gruyère cheese, grated
- ○ 60g (2¼ oz) butter
- ○ 15ml (1 tbls) flour
- ○ 200ml (7 fl oz) double cream
- ○ salt and pepper

1. Poach the cod fillets for 5 minutes in boiling water. Flake the flesh. Scrub and wash the mussels. Place them in a saucepan over a high heat until they open. Drain and remove them from their shells. Shell the prawns.
2. Clean and prepare the spinach. Cook in boiling salted water for 15 minutes. Drain thoroughly and chop roughly.
3. Prepare the sauce: melt 50g (2 oz) butter in a saucepan over a low heat. Add the flour, stir well, then add the cream. Season. Cook for 10 minutes until it thickens; remove from the heat.
4. Heat the grill. Mix together the spinach, mussels, prawns, cod fillets and sauce. Butter an ovenproof dish with the remaining butter and pour in the shellfish mixture. Sprinkle with Gruyère and cook until brown, 10 to 15 minutes.

A useful method for checking whether live shellfish are fresh is to squeeze the juice of a lemon over them. If they are fresh it will cause them to contract.

Tourteaux Farcis

Stuffed Crabs

Serves 4. Preparation: 35 min Cooking: 40 min

★★★

- ○ **4 live crabs**
- ○ **10ml (2 tsp) curry powder**
- ○ **6 tomatoes**
- ○ **40g (1¾ oz) butter**
- ○ **salt and pepper**

For the court-bouillon:
- ○ **240ml (9 fl oz) white wine**
- ○ **1 onion, studded with 4 cloves**
- ○ **2 carrots**
- ○ **5ml (1 tsp) peppercorns**
- ○ **5ml (1 tsp) coarse salt**
- ○ **1 bouquet garni consisting of:
  1 sprig thyme, 2 bay leaves, 3
  sprigs parsley**

1. Prepare the stock: in a large saucepan, place 2 litres (3½ pints) water, coarse salt, peppercorns, bouquet garni, onion, white wine and carrots. Bring to the boil, reduce the heat and simmer for 30 minutes.
2. Meanwhile, bring some water to the boil in another saucepan and immerse the tomatoes for 10 seconds. Drain, peel and remove the seeds. Melt 30g (1¼ oz) butter in a frying pan, add the tomatoes and mash them with a fork. Simmer for 20 minutes.
3. Preheat the oven to 250°C (475°F; gas mark 9).
4. Plunge the crabs into the stock. As soon as the stock returns to the boil, let them cook for 5 minutes, then remove from the heat. Leave to cool in the stock. Remove the white meat from the legs and claws, scrape off the brown meat, orange meat (the liver) and eggs (if any). Finely chop the crabmeat. Wash the shells and reserve.
5. Add the crabmeat to the tomatoes, stir well with a fork, add curry powder, season with salt and pepper and stir again. Cook for 1 minute.
6. Spoon the mixture into the shells, top with small knobs of butter and cook for 5 minutes. Serve at once.

Moules au Lard

Mussels with Bacon

Serves 6. Preparation: 15 min Cooking: 30 min

★

- ○ **3 litres (6½ lb) mussels**
- ○ **250g (9 oz) smoked bacon**
- ○ **100ml (3½ fl oz) double cream**
- ○ **1 large onion**
- ○ **2 carrots**
- ○ **2 bay leaves**
- ○ **240ml (9 fl oz) white wine**
- ○ **30g (1¼ oz) butter**
- ○ **pepper**

1. Scrub and wash the mussels and scrape off the beard-like strands and barnacles on the shells. Rinse well under cold running water and drain.
2. Dice the bacon, having removed the rind.
3. Melt the butter in a saucepan over a low heat. Fry the bacon for 15 minutes.
4. Peel the onion and chop finely. Peel and slice the carrots. Add the onion, carrots and bay leaves to the bacon. Season with pepper. Fry for 5 minutes, stirring occasionally.
5. Pour in the white wine. Add the mussels. After they start to open, shake the saucepan a few times. Cook until they have all opened.
6. Place the mussels in a dish, keeping their juice. Strain and blend with the cream. Pour the sauce over the mussels and serve immediately.

Soufflé aux Épinards

Serves 5. Preparation: 15 min Cooking: 1 hr

Spinach Soufflé

★★

- ○ **400g (14 oz) fresh spinach**
- ○ **50g (2 oz) grated Gruyère cheese**
- ○ **5 eggs**
- ○ **10g (½ oz) butter**
- ○ **salt and pepper**

For the white sauce (béchamel):
- ○ **50g (2 oz) butter**
- ○ **30g (1¼ oz) flour**
- ○ **240ml (9 fl oz) milk**
- ○ **15ml (1 tbls) double cream**
- ○ **1 pinch grated nutmeg**
- ○ **salt and pepper**

1. Preheat the oven to 140°C (275°F; gas mark 1).
2. Cut off the stalks of the spinach. Wash the leaves well. Plunge them into a saucepan filled with salted water and cook for 20 minutes.
3. Prepare a béchamel: melt the butter in a saucepan over a low heat, blend in the flour, stir well and cook until the flour and butter start to froth without colouring. Add the cold milk, a little at a time, stirring constantly with a wooden spoon, and cook for 15 minutes. Season, add the nutmeg and double cream. Stir and put aside.
4. Drain the spinach, and press it with a spoon to remove all the water. Chop roughly.
5. Separate the eggs. Beat the whites until stiff.
6. Mix the spinach with the béchamel, then add the egg yolks and grated Gruyère. Season to taste. Fold in the egg whites as gently as possible.
7. Butter a soufflé dish or mould, and fill with the spinach mixture. The dish should be almost three-quarters full. Place in the oven for 15 minutes at 140°C, then turn the heat up to 200°C (400°F; gas mark 6) and cook for a further 10 minutes. Serve at once.

Soufflé aux Blettes

Serves 4. Preparation: 20 min Cooking: 1 hr 10 min

Chard Soufflé

- ○ **1 bundle chard**
- ○ **150g (5 oz) smoked bacon**
- ○ **4 eggs**
- ○ **50g (2 oz) grated Gruyère cheese**
- ○ **20g (¾ oz) butter**
- ○ **salt and pepper**

For the white sauce (béchamel):
- ○ **50g (2 oz) butter**
- ○ **30g (1¼ oz) flour**
- ○ **240ml (9 fl oz) milk**
- ○ **15ml (1 tbls) double cream**
- ○ **1 pinch grated nutmeg**
- ○ **salt and pepper**

1. Preheat the oven to 140°C (275°F; gas mark 1).
2. Clean and prepare the chard by removing the threads and wash under running water. Cook for 20 minutes in salted water.
3. Prepare the white sauce: melt the butter in a saucepan over a low heat, and add the flour, stirring. Do not let it colour. Add the cold milk a little at a time, stirring constantly with a wooden spoon and cook for 15 minutes. Season, add the nutmeg and double cream. Stir well and put aside.
4. Dice the bacon, having removed the rind. Melt 10g (½ oz) butter in a frying pan over a medium heat, and fry the bacon for 10 minutes.
5. When the chard is cooked, drain well and chop roughly.
6. Separate the eggs. Beat the whites until stiff.
7. Mix the chard into the egg yolks, diced bacon, cheese and béchamel. Season. Gently fold in the egg whites.
8. Butter a soufflé dish or mould. Turn the chard mixture into it and cook in the oven for 15 minutes at 140°C, then turn the heat up to 200°C (400°F; gas mark 6) and cook for a further 10 minutes. Serve at once.

Egg whites, beaten until stiff, make a soufflé expand and attain its lightness. The success of the soufflé will depend on how stiffly the whites have been beaten, and also how lightly they have been folded into the body of the soufflé. When folding in the egg whites, make sure they retain as much of their volume as possible by cutting quickly into the soufflé mixture, from top to bottom, with a wooden spatula.

Soufflé au Fromage
Cheese Soufflé

Serves 4. Preparation: 20 min Cooking: 40 min

- ○ **15ml (1 tbls) double cream**
- ○ **4 eggs**
- ○ **150g (5 oz) grated Gruyère cheese**
- ○ **2 pinches grated nutmeg**
- ○ **10g (½ oz) butter**
- ○ **salt and pepper**

For the white sauce (béchamel):
- ○ **50g (2 oz) butter**
- ○ **30g (1¼ oz) flour**
- ○ **240ml (9 fl oz) milk**
- ○ **15ml (1 tbls) double cream**
- ○ **1 pinch grated nutmeg**
- ○ **salt and pepper**

1. Preheat the oven to 140°C (275°F; gas mark 1).
2. Prepare the béchamel: melt the butter in a saucepan over a low heat. Blend in the flour, stirring well, but do not let it colour. Add the milk a little at a time, stirring constantly with a wooden spoon, and cook for 15 minutes. Season. Add the nutmeg and cream. Stir well and leave to cool.
3. Separate the eggs. Add the yolks to the béchamel, one at a time. Season and add nutmeg, cheese and cream. Stir well. Beat the egg whites until stiff and fold them gently into the béchamel.
4. Butter a soufflé dish or mould, turn the mixture into the mould and bake for 15 minutes at 140°C. Then turn the heat up to 200°C (400°F; gas mark 6) and cook for a further 10 minutes. Serve at once.

Soufflé de Saumon
Salmon Soufflé

Serves 6. Preparation: 10 min Cooking: 45 min

- ○ **600g (21 oz) salmon steak**
- ○ **200ml (7 fl oz) double cream**
- ○ **6 egg whites**
- ○ **10g (½ oz) butter**
- ○ **salt and pepper**

1. Preheat the oven to 140°C (275°F; gas mark 1).
2. Grill the salmon steak for 10 minutes on each side. Remove the bones and flake the flesh. Season and put aside in a bowl.
3. Beat 2 egg whites until stiff, and fold into the salmon a little at a time, using a spatula. Work gently until the mixture is smooth. Beat the remaining 4 egg whites until stiff. Whip the cream lightly.
4. Gently stir the cream into the salmon mixture, then fold in the remaining egg whites as lightly as possible.
5. Butter a soufflé dish or mould, and pour the salmon mixture into the dish. Bake at 140°C for 15 minutes. Then turn the heat up to 200°C (400°F; gas mark 6) and cook for a further 10 minutes. Serve at once.

Soufflé de Morue
Salt Cod Soufflé

Serves 4. Preparation: 20 min Cooking: 50 min

★★

- ○ **600g (21 oz) filleted salt cod (previously soaked for 24 hrs)**
- ○ **600g (21 oz) potatoes**
- ○ **400ml (14 fl oz) double cream**
- ○ **110g (4¼ oz) butter**
- ○ **1 pinch cayenne pepper**
- ○ **1 pinch grated nutmeg**
- ○ **4 eggs**
- ○ **pepper**

1. Preheat the oven to 140°C (275°F; gas mark 1).
2. Bring some water to the boil and poach the cod fillets for 5 minutes. Drain and remove bones and skin. Put the meat aside.
3. Peel the potatoes and cook them for 20 minutes in salted water (or for 10 minutes in a pressure cooker).
4. Mash the potatoes and chop the cod as finely as possible, or mince in an electric mincer. Separate the eggs. Mix together the mashed potatoes, minced cod, cream, egg yolks, butter, cayenne pepper and nutmeg. Season lightly with pepper. Mix well.
5. Beat the egg whites until stiff.
6. Fold the egg whites lightly into the soufflé mixture. Butter a soufflé dish and fill it three-quarters full. Cook in the oven at 140°C for 15 minutes, then turn the heat up to 200°C (400°F; gas mark 6) and cook for a further 10 minutes. Serve at once.

Aspic de Poulet (p49) ▶

Soufflé à l'Oseille

Serves 4. Preparation: 20 min Cooking: 50 min

Sorrel Soufflé

★★

○ **250g (9 oz) fresh sorrel**
○ **4 eggs**
○ **20g (¾ oz) butter**
○ **10 tarragon leaves or chives**
○ **salt and pepper**

For the white sauce (béchamel):
○ **50g (2 oz) butter**
○ **30g (1¼ oz) flour**
○ **240ml (9 fl oz) milk**
○ **15ml (1 tbls) double cream**
○ **1 pinch grated nutmeg**
○ **salt and pepper**

1. Preheat the oven to 140°C (275°F; gas mark 1).
2. Discard the stalks of the sorrel, wash and dry the leaves. Wash and remove the stems of the tarragon (if using chives, wash and trim, and cut into small pieces).
3. Melt the butter in a saucepan. Add the sorrel, and cook over a low heat for 10 minutes. Remove from the heat and add the tarragon leaves (or chives). Season and mix well.
4. Prepare the béchamel: melt the butter in a saucepan over a low heat. Add the flour and stir well. Do not allow to colour. Then add the milk a little at a time, stirring all the time with a wooden spoon, and cook for 15 minutes. Season. Add the nutmeg and cream. Stir well and put aside.
5. Separate the eggs. Beat the whites until stiff.
6. In a bowl, mix together the sorrel, béchamel and egg yolks. Lightly fold in the egg whites.
7. Butter a soufflé dish or mould, and pour in the sorrel mixture. Bake at 140°C for 15 minutes and then turn the heat up to 200°C (400°F; gas mark 6) and cook for a further 10 minutes. Serve at once, with a mushroom salad.

Soufflé aux Fruits de Mer

Serves 5. Preparation: 40 min Cooking: 1 hr 15 min

Seafood Soufflé

★★

○ **1 litre (2½ lb) mussels**
○ **1 litre (2½ lb) cockles**
○ **200g (7 oz) button mushrooms**
○ **120ml (4 fl oz) white wine**
○ **100ml (3½ fl oz) double cream**
○ **5ml (1 tsp) tomato purée**
○ **2 pinches cayenne pepper**
○ **1 bouquet garni consisting of:**
    1 sprig thyme, 1 bay leaf, 3 sprigs parsley
○ **1 onion studded with 4 cloves**
○ **205g (7¼ oz) butter**
○ **90g (3½ oz) flour**
○ **240ml (9 fl oz) milk**
○ **4 eggs**
○ **100g (4 oz) prawns**
○ **1 pinch grated nutmeg**
○ **salt and pepper**

1. Preheat the oven to 200°C (400°F; gas mark 6).
2. Melt 100g (4 oz) butter in a saucepan over a low heat. Add 60g (2¼ oz) flour, stir well and cook until it froths, but do not allow to colour. Add the milk a little at a time, stirring. Bring to the boil, stirring constantly to avoid lumps. Cook until the sauce thickens. Separate the eggs. Remove the saucepan from the heat and stir in the egg yolks. Shell the prawns, and add them to the sauce. Season and add the nutmeg.
3. Beat the egg whites until stiff. Pour the soufflé mixture in a buttered soufflé dish or mould and gently fold in the egg whites. Place the mould into a shallow dish filled with water (*bain-marie*) and cook in the oven for 1 hour, or until cooked.
4. While the soufflé is cooking, scrub and wash the mussels and cockles well to remove the grit. Place them in a saucepan over a high heat, and cook until they open. Wash and trim the base of the mushrooms and fry gently in 30g (1¼ oz) butter, ensuring that they do not lose too much liquid.
5. Keep ½ litre (18 fl oz) of the juices from the mussels and cockles. Strain this liquid through a fine sieve. Prepare a court-bouillon or stock with this liquid, the white wine, onion and bouquet garni. Cook for 30 minutes.
6. Remove the mussels and cockles from their shells and put aside. Prepare a light roux by mixing the remaining flour with 75g (3 oz) melted butter, stirring all the time. Do not allow to brown. Strain the court-bouillon through a fine sieve and pour it slowly into the roux, stirring all the time. When the sauce has thickened, add the cream, tomato purée and cayenne pepper. Season with pepper and add the shellfish and mushrooms. Mix well. When the soufflé is ready, remove from the mould and pour the sauce over it. Serve at once.

Gelée de Viande: recette de base

Serves 6. Preparation and cooking: 7 hr

Home-made Jellied Consommé: basic recipe

★★

○ 1 calf's foot
○ 1 veal knuckle weighing 500g (18 oz)
○ 2 chicken wings
○ 2 chicken legs
○ 2 carrots
○ 2 onions
○ 4 cloves
○ 2 bay leaves
○ 2 sprigs thyme
○ 2 egg whites
○ 120ml (4 fl oz) white wine or Madeira
○ 6 peppercorns
○ coarse salt

1. Peel the onions and carrots. Wash the carrots and stud 1 onion with 4 cloves. Add some coarse salt to a saucepan filled with 3 litres (5¼ pints) water. Add the calf's foot and veal knuckle, the chicken wings and legs, bay leaves, sprigs of thyme and peppercorns. Bring to the boil and cook over a low heat for 6 to 7 hours. Skim the stock from time to time.
2. Place some ice cubes in the bottom of a saucepan and strain the stock through a sieve onto the ice cubes (to ensure that the fat sets). Repeat this operation a few times.
3. Put the jellied stock back in the pan over a low heat and add the egg whites, lightly beaten. Stir gently until it froths. Strain a few times through a fine sieve and add the white wine. Pour the jelly into a bowl. Leave to cool, then place in the refrigerator to set, or use it for a recipe in aspic.

Aspic de Poulet

Serves 4. Preparation: 20 min Cooking: 10 min
Refrigeration: 3 hr

Chicken in Aspic

★★★

○ 300g (10 oz) cooked chicken meat
○ 100g (4 oz) cooked ham
○ 60ml (4 tbls) oil
○ juice of ½ lemon
○ 1 packet aspic jelly powder or home-made jellied consommé
○ 3 gherkins
○ 12 stuffed green olives
○ 1 egg
○ 1 red pepper
○ 1 green pepper
○ salt and pepper

1. Place a savarin mould or a similar, ring-shaped mould in the freezer.
2. Remove the skin from the chicken and cut the flesh into small strips. Shred the ham similarly. Pour the oil and lemon juice over the strips of meat, season with salt and pepper and cover. Leave for 2 hours.
3. Dissolve the aspic jelly powder in lukewarm water (according to packet directions), or, if you are using home-made jellied consommé, soften it *au bain-marie*. Pour a layer 1cm (slightly less than ½ inch) thick at the bottom of the mould and allow to set by placing in the freezer for a short time.
4. Meanwhile, slice the gherkins and olives. Put aside 6 olive slices. Cut the peppers into strips, having removed the seeds. Add these ingredients to the chicken and ham. Pour over 30ml (2 tbls) of lukewarm aspic jelly and mix well. Hard boil the egg for 10 minutes. Shell and slice it.
5. Place 6 egg slices at the bottom of the mould, with slices of olives in between. Add the chicken mixture carefully, evening it out with the back of a spoon. Leave at least 1cm (slightly less than ½ in) of space between the mixture and the sides of the mould for the aspic jelly. Pour the rest of the aspic jelly gently into the space on the sides and on top of the chicken and ham mixture. Set in the refrigerator for 2 to 3 hours. To unmould, plunge the mould in hot water for a few seconds.

Gelées or jellies are used to coat, decorate or moisten pâtés or terrines. For a jellied fish stock, cook the heads, bones and trimmings of fish in water for a few hours (halibut, whiting or plaice are recommended). Bring to a boil, then skim and simmer uncovered. Strain the stock, which will set when it cools. To get a thicker jelly, simply add a little gelatine. You can flavour it with Madeira, port, lemon juice or white wine.

Aspics de Fruits de Mer

Seafood in Aspic

Serves 6. Preparation and cooking: 1 hr
Refrigeration: 3 hr 30 min
★ ★ ★

For the court-bouillon:
- 240ml (9 fl oz) white wine
- 1 bouquet garni consisting of: 2 bay leaves, 1 sprig thyme, 2 sprigs parsley
- salt, peppercorns

For the garnish:
- 500g (18 oz) king prawns
- 100g (4 oz) prawns
- 2 litres (4½ lb) mussels
- 2 packets fish jelly (if available, otherwise substitute 2 packets unflavoured gelatine and use fish stock instead of water)
- few strips of green and red peppers

1. Dissolve the fish jelly in lukewarm water (according to packet directions) and leave to cool. Place 6 small moulds or ramekins in the freezer for a few minutes.
2. Prepare a court-bouillon: in a saucepan, bring to the boil 1 litre (1¾ pints) water with the white wine. Season with salt, add the peppercorns and bouquet garni. Cook the court-bouillon for 15 minutes, then add both kinds of prawns. Cook for 3 minutes. Drain and put the prawns aside.
3. Scrub and wash the mussels well. Drain and place them in a saucepan over a high heat until they open. Remove the mussels from their shells and put aside.
4. Pour a little of the jelly, half set, into the small moulds. Place in the freezer. Meanwhile, shell the prawns.
5. When the jelly has set in the moulds, garnish with the pepper strips, a layer of prawns, a layer of mussels and another of prawns, with a little aspic jelly in between each layer. Each time that you make a jelly layer, place the moulds in the freezer for 10 minutes to allow to set. Finish with a thick layer of jelly, filling the mould to the top. Set in the freezer until firm. To unmould, plunge the moulds in hot water for a few seconds.

Aspic de Légumes

Vegetables in Aspic

Serves 4. Preparation and cooking: 35 min
Refrigeration: 3 hr
★ ★

- 5 firm tomatoes
- 1 cucumber
- 1 fennel
- 20 black olives
- 1 egg
- 1 slice ham (Parma or Bayonne style)
- 10 fresh mint leaves
- 1 bunch radishes
- 60ml (4 tbls) olive oil
- juice of 1 lemon
- 2 packets aspic jelly powder
- salt and pepper

1. Dissolve the aspic jelly powder in a little lukewarm water. Place a charlotte or similar mould in the freezer for a few minutes.
2. Immerse the tomatoes in boiling water for 10 seconds to peel them, then slice and remove the seeds. Peel the cucumber, remove the seeds with a knife and slice. Cut off the ends of the fennel, wash and dice. Stone the olives. Trim and slice the radishes. Cut the ham into small strips.
3. Place all the ingredients except the ham in a bowl. Pour over the olive oil and lemon juice, season and mix well. Put aside.
4. Meanwhile, hard boil the egg for 10 minutes. Shell and slice. Pour a little of the aspic jelly, half set, into the bottom of the mould and place in the freezer. Wash and dry the mint leaves.
5. At the bottom of the mould place the egg slices, alternating with the mint leaves. Cover with some of the vegetable mixture, leaving a small space in between the sides of the mould and the vegetable mixture. Add a layer of ham and finish with another layer of vegetable mixture. Pour the remaining jelly slowly around the mixture and set in the refrigerator for 2 to 3 hours.

You can serve this dish with a simple lettuce salad accompanied by a cream and egg sauce. For the sauce, hard boil 3 eggs for 10 minutes, shell them and remove and mash the egg yolks. Add 60ml (4 tbls) cream to the egg yolks. Mix well and add 30ml (2 tbls) oil and 15ml (1 tbls) vinegar (wine vinegar preferably). Season and mix well. Just before serving, add the lettuce leaves and toss.

Aspics d'Huîtres

Oysters in Aspic

Serves 4. Preparation: 25 min
Refrigeration: 4 hr
★★★

○ **4 dozen oysters**
○ **120ml (8 tbls) mayonnaise**
○ **2 packets fish gelatine (or
substitute 2 packets
unflavoured gelatine and use
fish stock instead of water)**

1. Dissolve the gelatine in lukewarm water. Pour a thin layer of jelly at the bottom of 4 ramekins and place in the freezer for a few minutes.
2. Open the oysters and discard the shells. Pour their juices into a saucepan, bring to the boil, and plunge the oysters in the liquid for 30 seconds.
3. Prepare some mustardy mayonnaise.
4. Place a layer of oysters at the bottom of the moulds, cover with a layer of mayonnaise and then a layer of aspic jelly. Place in the refrigerator. Repeat this operation until the moulds are filled. Cover with the rest of the aspic jelly. Leave in the refrigerator for at least 3 hours. To unmould, plunge the moulds in hot water for a few seconds.

Instead of oysters, you can follow this recipe using the white flesh and coral of scallops.

Aspics de Colin

Hake in Aspic

Serves 4. Preparation: 25 min Cooking: 35 min
Refrigeration: 3 hr
★★

○ **6 courgettes**
○ **2 red peppers**
○ **500g (18 oz) hake**
○ **1 egg**
○ **45ml (3 tbls) oil**
○ **juice of 1 lemon**
○ **1 clove garlic**
○ **1 handful chives**
○ **1 packet aspic jelly powder**
○ **salt and pepper**

For the court-bouillon:
○ **2 carrots**
○ **1 onion, studded with 4 cloves**
○ **1 bouquet garni consisting of:
1 sprig thyme, 2 sprigs parsley,
1 bay leaf**
○ **120ml (4 fl oz) white wine**
○ **coarse salt, peppercorns**

1. Prepare a court-bouillon: peel the carrots and cut them lengthways. In a saucepan filled with salted water, place the carrots, onion, bouquet garni, white wine and peppercorns. Simmer for 20 minutes. Place a savarin or similar mould in the freezer for a few minutes.
2. Slice the courgettes (1cm/½ inch thick). Trim the peppers, remove the seeds and cut into strips. Bring some water to the boil. Cook the courgettes and peppers in boiling water for 15 minutes. Drain. Prepare a sauce: peel and crush the garlic. In a bowl, dissolve the salt in the lemon juice. Add the oil and garlic, season with pepper and stir well. Add the courgettes and peppers and mix well. Place the bowl in the refrigerator.
3. Plunge the hake in the court-bouillon. When it starts to boil, turn off the heat and leave to cool for 10 minutes. Remove the fish with a skimmer. Strain the court-bouillon through a fine sieve and dissolve the aspic jelly powder in the stock. Pour a little of the jellied stock into the bottom of the mould. Leave to set in the freezer. Remove the skin from the hake and cut into pieces.
4. Place a layer of peppers and courgettes at the bottom of the mould, putting aside 15 slices of courgette. Top with a layer of hake, with another layer of peppers and courgettes on top. Pour on the rest of the jellied stock, filling the mould to the top. Leave in the refrigerator for 3 hours.
5. Before unmoulding, hard boil 1 egg for 10 minutes. Shell and mash with a fork.
6. Unmould the aspic onto a serving dish. Garnish with the remaining slices of courgettes, and sprinkle with chopped chives and mashed egg. Serve at once.

Hake can be replaced by saithe, cod, mackerel, salmon, etc. Instead of courgettes, try substituting cauliflower or cabbage or a combination of cucumbers and tomatoes, all cut into shreds.

Mousse de Tomates

Serves 4. Preparation: 15 min

Tomato Mousse

★

○ **2kg (4½ lb) red, ripe tomatoes**
○ **1 small clove garlic**
○ **200ml (7 fl oz) double cream**
○ **2 sprigs fresh basil or parsley**
○ **salt and pepper**

1. Bring some water to the boil and immerse the tomatoes for 10 seconds. Drain, peel and remove the seeds. Mash with a fork and pour away any excess juice.
2. Peel and chop the garlic. Pass the tomatoes and garlic through the fine mesh of a vegetable mill (or use a liquidizer). Season.
3. Place some ice cubes in a deep dish. Place a smaller bowl inside. Pour the cream into the bowl and whip. Fold the cream gently into the tomato purée. Pour the mousse into 4 ramekins and refrigerate. Just before serving, sprinkle with the basil leaves or chopped parsley.

Mousse de Jambon

Serves 4. Preparation: 20 min Cooking: 45 min

Ham Mousse

★★

○ **500g (18 oz) cooked ham**
○ **200ml (7 fl oz) double cream**
○ **2 pinches paprika**
○ **2 egg whites**
○ **10g (½ oz) butter**
○ **salt and pepper**

1. Preheat the oven to 200°C (400°F; gas mark 6).
2. Pass the ham through a vegetable mill or an electric mincer. Beat the egg whites until stiff.
3. Whip the cream. In a bowl, gently mix the cream with the minced ham. Add 2 pinches paprika and season lightly with salt and pepper. Fold in the egg whites gently.
4. Butter a charlotte or similar mould and pour in the ham mixture. Place the mould in an ovenproof dish filled with water and cook for 40 to 45 minutes. When the contents of the mould begin to rise and puff up, the mousse is cooked. Remove from the oven. Wait a few minutes while the mousse sinks slightly, then turn onto a serving dish. Wait 2 to 3 minutes, then unmould.

Mousse de Cervelle à l'Oseille

Serves 6. Preparation and cooking: 1 hr 30 min
Refrigeration: 1 hr

Mousse of Brains and Sorrel

★★

○ **4 lamb's brains**
○ **400g (14 oz) sorrel**
○ **100g (4 oz) butter**
○ **200ml (7 fl oz) double cream**
○ **1 jar (50g/2 oz) stuffed olives**
○ **juice of ½ lemon**

For the court-bouillon:
○ **½ litre (18 fl oz) dry white wine**
○ **2 peeled onions**
○ **4 cloves**
○ **2 peeled carrots**
○ **2 peeled cloves garlic**
○ **bouquet garni consisting of: thyme, bay leaves, parsley**
○ **salt and pepper**

1. Prepare the stock: add all the ingredients for the court-bouillon to ½ litre (18 fl oz) water and bring to the boil. Simmer for 30 minutes. Meanwhile, soak the brains in cold water for approximately 30 minutes.
2. When the court-bouillon is ready, strain it through a sieve and put aside to cool. Remove the fibres and all traces of blood from the brains. Drain and place them in the court-bouillon. Poach over a low heat for 20 minutes.
3. Wash the sorrel and cut off the stalks. Melt 50g (2 oz) butter in a frying pan and cook the sorrel leaves for 10 minutes. Remove the brains from the stock and drain. Fry them gently in another frying pan with the remaining butter for 5 minutes. Do not allow to brown.
4. Mince the brains and sorrel in a liquidizer or mincer, or push them through a sieve. Mix well and add the lemon juice. Whip the cream until stiff and then fold, a little at a time, into the brain and sorrel mixture. Pour the mousse into ramekins and garnish with olives. Refrigerate for 1 hour before serving.

Mousse d'Artichauts

Mousse of Artichoke Hearts

Serves 4. Preparation: 15 min

○ **1 tin (220g/7¾ oz) artichoke hearts**
○ **200ml (7 fl oz) double cream**
○ **10g (½ oz) pistachio nuts**
○ **1 small green pepper**
○ **salt and pepper**

1. Drain the artichoke hearts and dice. Mix them with 15ml (1 tbls) cream and liquidize or pass them through the fine mesh of a vegetable mill. Pour this mixture into a bowl. Whip the remaining cream and fold delicately into the artichoke mixture. Season.
2. Remove the seeds from the pepper and dice. Shell and skin the pistachios, easing off the skins by pinching each nut between thumb and forefinger.
3. Pour the artichoke mousse into 4 ramekins and garnish with the pistachio nuts and diced pepper. Refrigerate before serving.

Mousse d'Avocats

Avocado Mousse

Serves 4. Preparation: 10 min

★

○ **2 avocados**
○ **45ml (3 tbls) double cream**
○ **5ml (1 tsp) cognac**
○ **juice of 1 lemon**
○ **salt and pepper**

1. Halve the avocados and remove the stones. With a spoon, carefully scoop out the flesh, reserving the skins.
2. In a liquidizer, place the avocado flesh, cream, lemon juice and cognac. Season. Blend until smooth.
3. Fill the avocado skins with the mousse. Refrigerate and serve very cold.

Mousse de Faisan en Aspic

Pheasant Mousse in Aspic

Serves 4. Preparation: 20 min Cooking: 40 min
Refrigeration: 2 hr
★ ★ ★

○ **1 pheasant**
○ **45ml (3 tbls) oil**
○ **4 sheets gelatine**
○ **120ml (4 fl oz) Madeira**
○ **200ml (7 fl oz) double cream**
○ **30g (1¼ oz) butter**
○ **salt and pepper**

1. Preheat the oven to 200°C (400°F; gas mark 6). Rub the inside of the pheasant with salt and pepper. Rub the outside with oil and butter. Roast for 40 minutes, basting with the cooking juices from time to time.
2. Remove the skin and bone the pheasant. Chop the flesh, then mince with the cream in an electric mincer or liquidizer. Season to taste, if necessary.
3. In a bowl, soak the sheets of gelatine in ¼ litre (9 fl oz) lukewarm water and the Madeira. Leave to cool.
4. Pour some of this liquid into a terrine or mould, brushing it onto the sides. Place in the freezer until set.
5. Pour the pheasant mousse into the terrine and cover with the remainder of the jellied liquid. Leave to set in the refrigerator for 2 hours. To unmould, dip the terrine into a bowl of hot water for a few seconds.

This mousse may be accompanied by an onion mousse. Peel 500g (18 oz) onions and fry them over a low heat with 100g (4 oz) smoked bacon, cut into strips. Add a glass of water and cover the pan. Cook for 30 minutes. If necessary add a little water to prevent the onions from sticking to the pan. Reduce the onions to a purée in a vegetable mill or liquidizer. Add 45ml (3 tbls) whipped cream to the purée and season. You can serve this onion mousse either hot or cold.

Mousse de Saumon

Salmon Mousse

Serves 4. Preparation: 20 min Cooking: 25 min
Refrigeration: 1 hr
★ ★

○ **300g (10 oz) fresh salmon**
○ **75ml (5 tbls) double cream**
○ **juice of 1 lemon**
○ **100g (4 oz) prawns**
○ **10 small sprigs chervil, coarsely chopped**

For the court-bouillon:
○ **¼ litre (9 fl oz) white wine**
○ **1 bouquet garni consisting of: 1 sprig thyme, 2 bay leaves, 3 sprigs parsley**
○ **1 peeled onion, studded with 4 cloves**
○ **5ml (1 tsp) peppercorns**
○ **5ml (1 tsp) coarse salt**

1. Prepare the court-bouillon: pour into a saucepan ½ litre (18 fl oz) water. Add the white wine, bouquet garni, onion, peppercorns and coarse salt. Cook for 20 minutes. Plunge the salmon into the court-bouillon and when it starts to boil, remove from the heat and leave to cool for 5 minutes. Drain the salmon and remove the bones and skin. Flake the flesh.
2. Shell the prawns and put aside.
3. In a liquidizer, blend the salmon and lemon juice. Whip the cream and fold delicately into the salmon purée. Pour the mousse into 4 ramekins and refrigerate for 1 hour. Just before serving, garnish with the chervil and prawns.

This mousse can be served in aspic. You will need a packet of fish gelatine (or jellied fish stock), some sliced carrots and finely sliced gherkins. Place a mould in the refrigerator. If using fish gelatine, dissolve it in lukewarm water. Pour some jellied stock into the bottom of the mould and leave to set in the freezer. Mix 75ml (5 tbls) jellied stock with the salmon mousse. Place the sliced carrots and gherkins at the bottom of the mould and pour in the salmon mousse, leaving a small space between the mixture and the sides of the mould. Pour the remaining jellied stock into this space and on the top. Refrigerate for 2 to 3 hours until it sets. Cover a serving dish with lettuce leaves and unmould the mousse onto this.

Mousse de Crabe

Crab Mousse

Serves 4. Preparation: 15 min Cooking: 1 hr
★ ★

○ **1 tin (300g/10 oz) crabmeat**
○ **100g (4 oz) prawns**
○ **100g (4 oz) whiting fillets**
○ **2 egg yolks**
○ **¼ litre (9 fl oz) white wine**
○ **1 small onion**
○ **juice of 1 lemon**
○ **1 bay leaf**
○ **1 sprig thyme**
○ **75ml (5 tbls) double cream**
○ **20g (¾ oz) butter**
○ **salt and pepper**

1. Shell the prawns, keeping the shells for the stock. Peel the onion. In a saucepan, place the onion, prawn shells, bay leaf, sprig of thyme, white wine and ½ litre (18 fl oz) water. Season and cook over a medium heat for 20 minutes. Pass the stock through the fine mesh of a vegetable mill and put back on the heat.
2. Drain the crabmeat, removing any cartilage which may have been left in. Immerse the crabmeat and whiting fillets in the stock. When the stock starts to boil, remove from the heat and leave for 5 minutes. Drain.
3. Liquidize the crabmeat, whiting, prawns, lemon juice, egg yolks, and salt and pepper to taste.
4. Whip the cream and fold gently into the mousse. Butter 4 ramekins or small moulds and pour the mousse into each one. Cook *au bain-marie* for 35 minutes. Cool and unmould.

This mousse may be served with a *sauce verte*: mayonnaise mixed with a purée of chervil, spinach, tarragon or watercress (use one or a mixture of two or three). First blanch the chosen vegetables then squeeze dry and push through the fine mesh of a vegetable mill and blend with the mayonnaise.

Terrine de Légumes Verts

Serves 6. Preparation: 20 min Cooking: 1 hr 30 min

Terrine of Green Vegetables

★ ★ ★

- ○ **1 bundle chard**
- ○ **500g (18 oz) leeks**
- ○ **2 green peppers**
- ○ **500g (18 oz) spinach**
- ○ **1 cucumber**
- ○ **50g (2 oz) pistachio nuts**
- ○ **1 onion**
- ○ **100g (4 oz) butter**
- ○ **15ml (1 tbls) soya sauce**
- ○ **salt and pepper**

To seal the terrine:
- ○ **flour and water**

1. Prepare the vegetables: chop the chard and leeks. Halve the peppers, remove the seeds, and cut into strips. Cut the stalks off the spinach and wash the leaves well under running water. Peel the cucumber, remove the seeds and slice thinly. Peel and slice the onion, separating into rings.
2. Bring some salted water to the boil. Plunge the vegetables, one sort at a time, into the boiling water, blanching each for 10 minutes. Drain, keeping the different vegetables separate.
3. Melt 20g (¾ oz) butter in a frying pan and gently fry all the vegetables except the cucumber, one after the other, for 5 minutes each. Season and add a few drops of soya sauce to each vegetable a few seconds before removing from the heat.
4. Preheat the oven to 230°C (450°F; gas mark 8).
5. Butter a terrine or a large mould with the remaining butter. Fill with a layer of spinach, a layer of leeks, one of pepper, one of chard and so on, placing in between each layer the sliced cucumber, onion rings and pistachio nuts.
6. Cover the terrine and seal it with a strip of flour and water paste. Bake for 20 to 25 minutes. This may be eaten either hot or cold.

Terrine de Légumes d'Été

Serves 6. Preparation: 20 min Cooking: 35 min

Terrine of Summer Vegetables

★ ★

- ○ **4 aubergines**
- ○ **4 courgettes**
- ○ **1 head fennel**
- ○ **4 tomatoes**
- ○ **1 apple**
- ○ **1 red pepper**
- ○ **1 bunch fresh mint**
- ○ **15 fresh basil leaves**
- ○ **6 pinches cumin powder**
- ○ **1 lemon**
- ○ **60ml (4 tbls) olive oil**
- ○ **20g (¾ oz) butter**
- ○ **salt and pepper**

To seal the terrine:
- ○ **flour and water**

1. Prepare the vegetables: trim off the base of the fennel, cut into pieces, wash well and drain. Wash and halve the pepper, remove the seeds and cut into strips. Peel the aubergines and courgettes. Cut them lengthways into strips approximately ½cm (¼ inch) thick. Wash and slice the tomatoes.
2. Bring some water to the boil and blanch the fennel for 10 minutes. Drain.
3. Meanwhile, fry the aubergines and courgettes in the olive oil for 5 minutes. Drain on absorbent paper.
4. Peel and quarter the apple, remove the core and cut into thin slices. Wash and cut the lemon into thin slices, removing the pips.
5. Preheat the oven to 200°C (400°F; gas mark 6).
6. Butter a terrine or baking dish and put at the bottom a layer of tomatoes, then a layer of apple. Season. Add a pinch of cumin and a few mint leaves. Add a layer of courgettes, one of lemon slices, one of fennel, one of pepper, and one of aubergines, placing a few mint leaves, a pinch of cumin and salt and pepper to taste between each layer. Repeat until there is only 1cm (½ inch) space left on top.
7. Cover the terrine and seal it with a strip of flour and water paste. Bake for 20 to 25 minutes. Just before serving, open the terrine and sprinkle with fresh basil leaves. This dish is equally good hot or cold.

Poulet en Terrine

Chicken Terrine

Serves 6. Preparation: 30 min Cooking 2 hr 5 min

★ ★ ★

○ **1 chicken weighing approximately 1.2kg (2½ lb)**
○ **300g (10 oz) ham (Parma or Bayonne style)**
○ **150g (5 oz) thin rashers of unsmoked, fat streaky bacon**
○ **60ml (2 fl oz) cognac**
○ **250g (9 oz) pork fillet or lean pork**
○ **2 eggs**
○ **250g (9 oz) breast of veal**
○ **80g (3¼ oz) butter**
○ **4 pinches mixed spice**
○ **1 packet powdered gelatine**
○ **salt and pepper**

To seal the terrine:
○ **flour and water**

1. Bone the chicken and brown gently for 5 minutes in butter, stirring with a wooden spoon. Put aside.
2. Chop the pork, veal and ham, add the eggs and mixed spice, season and pour in the cognac. Dissolve the gelatine in ½ litre (18 fl oz) lukewarm water. Add to the pork mixture and mix well.
3. Preheat the oven to 200°C (400°F; gas mark 6).
4. Line the bottom of a terrine with half the bacon rashers. Cover with a layer of the pork mixture and then a layer of chicken, repeating until the terrine is completely filled. Cover with the remaining bacon rashers and then with the lid.
5. Seal the lid of the terrine with a strip of flour and water paste. Bake for 2 hours. When cold, refrigerate for 48 hours before serving.

You can serve this terrine with pickled onions, gherkins and small black or green olives.

Terrine de Rougets Grondins

Gurnard Terrine

Serves 8. Marinade: 1 hr 30 min
Preparation: 15 min Cooking: 1 hr 30 min

★ ★ ★

○ **8 fillets of gurnard**
○ **½ litre (18 fl oz) white wine**
○ **400ml (14 fl oz) double cream**
○ **4 sheets gelatine**
○ **3 eggs**
○ **50g (2 oz) pistachio nuts, shelled**
○ **50g (2 oz) thin rashers unsmoked, fat streaky bacon**
○ **15ml (1 tbls) parsley, stalks removed**
○ **5 sprigs chives, chopped**
○ **2 pinches mixed spice**
○ **salt and pepper**

To seal the terrine:
○ **flour and water**

1. Choose 4 gurnards and ask your fishmonger to remove the backbone.
2. Put aside 4 fillets and place them in a dish. Sprinkle with mixed spice and pour over the white wine. Marinate in the refrigerator for 1 hour.
3. Dissolve the gelatine in ½ litre (18 fl oz) lukewarm water.
4. Take the 4 remaining fillets and mince them or chop very finely. Mix with the eggs, cream, parsley, chives and gelatine dissolved in water. Season and mix well, then add the wine from the marinade and the pistachio nuts. Mix well and leave in the refrigerator for 30 minutes.
5. Preheat the oven to 170°C (325°F; gas mark 3).
6. Line the bottom of a terrine with the bacon rashers. Fill the terrine with half the minced fish mixture. Place 2 fillets on top, add the remaining mixture and cover with the 2 remaining fillets.
7. Cover the terrine and seal the lid with a strip of flour and water paste. Place the terrine in a large ovenproof dish filled with water and bake for 1½ hours. Let cool and serve at room temperature with a green salad or watercress purée.

Terrines or pâtés are cooked in deep baking dishes, usually made of glazed pottery, covered with a lid sealed with a paste made of a mixture of flour and water. Sealed, they will keep for 15 days in a refrigerator or a cool place.

Mousse de Saumon (p56) ▶

Terrine de Foies de Volaille

Chicken Liver Terrine

Serves 6-8. Preparation: 20 min Cooking: 2 hr

★ ★ ★

- ○ 1kg (2¼ lb) chicken livers
- ○ 350g (12 oz) fresh pork belly
- ○ 300g (10 oz) pig's liver
- ○ 500g (18 oz) boneless pork loin
- ○ 30ml (1 fl oz) cognac
- ○ 2 eggs
- ○ 150g (5 oz) thin rashers unsmoked, streaky bacon
- ○ 3 bay leaves
- ○ 30ml (2 tbls) powdered gelatine
- ○ 2 pinches mixed spice
- ○ salt and pepper

To seal the terrine:
- ○ flour and water

1. Mince the chicken livers, pork, pig's liver and loin as finely as possible. Dissolve the gelatine in ½ litre (18 fl oz) lukewarm water.
2. Mix all ingredients well and season highly.
3. Preheat the oven to 200°C (400°F; gas mark 6).
4. Fill a terrine with the mixture, place the bacon rashers on top and garnish with bay leaves. Cover with the lid and seal with a strip of flour and water paste.
5. Place the terrine in an ovenproof dish filled with water. Bake for 2 hours. Leave to cool in the oven and keep for 24 hours before serving.

Pâté de Foie de Porc

Pig's Liver Pâté

Serves 6-8. Preparation: 20 min Cooking: 2 hr

★ ★ ★

- ○ 1kg (2¼ lb) pig's liver
- ○ 500g (18 oz) fresh pork belly
- ○ 2 eggs
- ○ 15ml (1 tbls) flour
- ○ 50g (2 oz) caul fat
- ○ 150g (5 oz) barding fat
- ○ 150g (5 oz) fresh bacon, unsalted and unsmoked
- ○ 2 pinches mixed spice
- ○ salt and pepper

To seal the terrine:
- ○ flour and water

1. Remove any hard membranes or nerves from the liver. Finely mince the pork belly, the liver and 3 oz bacon. Add the flour and eggs, season well and add the mixed spice.
2. Cut the remaining bacon into small pieces and season.
3. Preheat the oven to 200°C (400°F; gas mark 6).
4. Spread the caul fat on the bottom of a terrine, cover with a layer of minced mixture, then a few pieces of bacon, then another layer of minced mixture and a few more pieces of bacon. Repeat, finishing with a layer of minced mixture. Place the barding fat on top and cover with the lid. Seal the terrine with a strip of flour and water paste.
5. Place the terrine in a large ovenproof dish filled with water. Bake for 2 hours. Cool and refrigerate for 48 hours before serving.

Pâté de Faisan

Pheasant Pâté

Serves 6-8. Marinade: 1 hr
Preparation: 30 min Cooking: 2 hr

★ ★ ★

- ○ 1 good-sized pheasant
- ○ 200g (7 oz) breast of veal
- ○ 200g (7 oz) fresh bacon, unsmoked and unsalted
- ○ 2 egg yolks
- ○ 2 pinches mixed spice
- ○ 80ml (3 fl oz) cognac
- ○ salt and pepper

To seal the terrine:
- ○ flour and water

1. Remove the meat from the pheasant and marinate the flesh in cognac for 1 hour in the refrigerator.
2. Put aside the pheasant breast. Chop the remaining pheasant flesh with the bacon and veal. Season, add the mixed spice and bind with the egg yolks.
3. Preheat the oven to 200°C (400°F; gas mark 6).
4. Place the chopped meat in the terrine, alternating with the slices of pheasant breast. Finish with a layer of chopped meat. Cover the terrine with the lid.
5. Seal the lid with a strip of paste made of flour and water. Bake in the centre of the oven, in a baking tin filled with water, for 2 hours. Let cool and refrigerate for 48 hours before serving.

Pâté de Lapin
Rabbit Pâté

Serves 6-8. Preparation: 30 min Cooking: 2 hr 30 min

- ○ 1 rabbit weighing 1.5kg (3¼ lb)
- ○ 300g (10 oz) breast of veal
- ○ 400g (14 oz) fresh bacon
- ○ 30ml (2 tbls) brandy
- ○ 150g (5 oz) barding fat or thin rashers of unsmoked, streaky bacon
- ○ 4 bay leaves
- ○ 2 pinches mixed spice
- ○ 1 carrot
- ○ 1 large onion
- ○ 1 bouquet garni consisting of: 1 sprig thyme, 1 bay leaf, 3 sprigs parsley
- ○ salt and pepper

To seal the terrine:
- ○ flour and water

1. Remove the meat from the rabbit. Peel the carrot and onion and slice. Remove the rind from the bacon. Put the rabbit bones in a saucepan with the carrot, onion, bacon rind and bouquet garni. Season. Cover with water and simmer until two-thirds of the liquid has evaporated. Strain the stock.
2. Choose 20 nice small fillets (10 each) from the rabbit and veal. Season and put aside.
3. Mince the remaining rabbit and veal with the bacon (preferably in an electric mincer). Season, and add the mixed spice and brandy. Mix with a wooden spatula, adding the stock a little at a time.
4. Preheat the oven to 200°C (400°F; gas mark 6).
5. Line a terrine with the barding fat or rashers of bacon. Place in alternate layers the minced and sliced meats, ending with a layer of minced meat. Cover with slices of barding fat or rashers of bacon and lay the bay leaves on the top. Cover the terrine with the lid and seal the lid with a strip of flour and water paste.
6. Bake in the centre of the oven, in an ovenproof dish filled with water, for 2 hours. Leave the lid on while the pâté cools. Refrigerate for a few days before serving.

Pâté d'Anguilles
Eel Pâté

Serves 8. Preparation: 40 min Cooking: 1 hr 30 min

- ○ 400g (14 oz) frozen shortcrust pastry
- ○ 2 eels weighing approximately 500g (18 oz) each
- ○ 200g (7 oz) shelled prawns
- ○ 6 fillets of whiting
- ○ 500g (18 oz) fresh spinach
- ○ 200g (7 oz) button mushrooms, thinly sliced
- ○ 60ml (4 tbls) double cream
- ○ juice of ½ lemon
- ○ 2 egg yolks
- ○ 120ml (4 fl oz) white wine
- ○ 4 pinches mixed spice
- ○ 45ml (3 tbls) fresh herbs, coarsely chopped: chives, parsley, chervil
- ○ 20g (¾ oz) butter
- ○ 1 packet powdered gelatine
- ○ salt and pepper

1. Thaw the pastry. Ask your fishmonger to clean and skin the eels. Cut 2 pieces (5cm/2 inches long) off the eels and put them aside. Chop the remaining flesh, as well as the fillets of whiting and the prawns.
2. In a bowl, mix the chopped fish and prawns with the mushrooms. Pour over the white wine and lemon juice. Add the cream, 1 egg yolk and the chopped herbs. Season and add the mixed spice. Mix well. Refrigerate.
3. Remove the spinach stalks and wash the leaves under running water. Drain and cut into strips.
4. Preheat the oven to 200°C (400°F; gas mark 6).
5. Roll out the pastry to a thickness of 5mm (¼ inch). Butter a pie dish and line it with three-quarters of the pastry, easing the pastry smoothly and evenly into the base and up the sides of the dish, extending slightly above the top. Cover with a layer of spinach, then a layer of the fish mixture, then the pieces of eel and another layer of the fish mixture. Finish with the remaining spinach.
6. Roll out the remaining pastry to form a lid. Cover the pâté, pinching the edges of the pastry together firmly. Glaze the top of the pie by brushing with the remaining egg yolk. Make a hole in the centre of the lid, and place a tiny roll of buttered paper in it to allow the steam to escape. Bake for 1½ hours. Remove from the oven and pour the gelatine, which you have dissolved in a few spoonfuls of lukewarm water, through the hole in the top of the pâté. Leave to cool for 24 hours before serving.

Boulettes de Jambon

Ham Croquettes

Serves 4. Preparation: 10 min Cooking: 10 min

★★

○ **250g (9 oz) white bread, crusts removed**
○ **240ml (9 fl oz) milk**
○ **150g (5 oz) ham (Parma or Bayonne style)**
○ **15ml (1 tbls) roughly chopped herbs: chervil, parsley, chives**
○ **2 eggs**
○ **50g (2 oz) butter**
○ **30g (1¼ oz) breadcrumbs**
○ **20g (¾ oz) flour**
○ **salt and pepper**

1. Soak the bread in the milk. Mash with a fork, then drain. In a bowl, mix the bread with the eggs until it becomes paste-like.
2. Mince the ham finely. Fry in 30g (1¼ oz) butter over a low heat. Add the chopped herbs. Mix with the bread paste and season to taste.
3. Bring some salted water to the boil in a large saucepan.
4. Form walnut-sized balls with the ham mixture and roll them in the flour. Plunge them in boiling water for 5 minutes. Drain. Fry the breadcrumbs in the remaining butter, then roll the croquettes in them.

You can serve these croquettes with grated Parmesan or Gruyère cheese.

Boulettes de Viande au Concombre

Meatballs with Cucumber

Serves 4. Preparation: 15 min
Cooking: 15 min
★

○ **250g (9 oz) minced beef (steak preferably)**
○ **1 egg**
○ **15ml (1 tbls) cornflour**
○ **15ml (1 tbls) dry white wine**
○ **half a cucumber**
○ **10 button mushrooms**
○ **salt and pepper**
○ **240ml (9 fl oz) oil for deep frying**

1. Peel the cucumber, remove the seeds and chop. Bring some water to the boil, blanch the cucumber pieces for 10 minutes and drain. Cut the earthy base off the mushrooms, wash and chop finely.
2. In a bowl mix the minced beef, egg, white wine, cornflour, chopped mushrooms and cucumber. Season, and mash all the ingredients well.
3. Form small balls with the mixture. Heat the oil, fry the balls for 5 minutes and drain on absorbent paper.

Boulettes de Fromage Blanc

Cream Cheese Croquettes

Serves 5. Preparation: 15 min Cooking: 15 min

★★

○ **500g (18 oz) fromage blanc or cream cheese**
○ **150g (5 oz) butter**
○ **50g (2 oz) flour**
○ **50g (2 oz) breadcrumbs**
○ **3 eggs**
○ **salt**

1. Drain the fromage blanc, if used. Melt 50g (2 oz) butter.
2. In a bowl, mix the flour, salt, eggs and cheese. Add the melted butter and mix well to obtain a smooth paste.
3. Bring some salted water to the boil in a large saucepan. Drop tablespoonfuls of the mixture into the boiling water.
4. As soon as they come to the surface of the water, remove the croquettes and drain in a colander. Separate them if they stick together.
5. Place the breadcrumbs on a plate and roll each croquette in them. Heat the remaining butter in a frying pan over a medium heat. Fry the croquettes for 3 minutes. They must be firm on the outside and soft inside.

Galettes de Fromage
Cream Cheese Cakes

Serves 6. Preparation: 10 min Cooking: 30 min

★★

○ **500g (18 oz) fromage blanc or cream cheese**
○ **4 eggs**
○ **1 bunch chives**
○ **200g (7 oz) flour**
○ **salt and pepper**
○ **200ml (7 fl oz) oil for deep frying**

1. Drain the fromage blanc, if used. Separate the eggs. Beat the whites until stiff.
2. Chop the chives finely. In a bowl, whisk gently together the fromage blanc, egg yolks, flour and chives. Season with salt and pepper.
3. Heat the oil in a frying pan. Meanwhile, fold the egg whites into the ingredients in the bowl.
4. Form the mixture into small balls and flatten with a fork. Fry them, a few at a time, in hot oil for 5 minutes on each side. As soon as each batch is cooked, drain and keep warm in a low oven.

Allumettes au Roquefort
Roquefort Sticks

Serves 4. Preparation: 10 min Cooking: 15 min

★★

○ **200g (7 oz) flour**
○ **150g (5 oz) Roquefort cheese**
○ **50g (2 oz) butter**
○ **200ml (7 fl oz) milk**
○ **salt and pepper**

1. Preheat the oven to 250°C (475°F; gas mark 9).
2. In a saucepan over a low heat, melt the butter and cheese. Stir well with a wooden spoon until the ingredients become paste-like.
3. Place the flour, milk and butter and Roquefort paste in a bowl. Season and knead into a ball. Roll out the dough on a flour-covered board to a thickness of ½cm (¼ inch).
4. With a knife, cut the dough into rectangles 4cm (1½ inches) wide and 10cm (4 inches) long. Butter a baking sheet.
5. Place the sticks on the baking sheet and bake for 15 minutes. Check from time to time. Do not allow them to get too brown. You can serve these Roquefort sticks hot or cold.

In the same way, you can prepare ham, almond or cumin sticks: mix the flour, milk, butter, salt and pepper. Then add either minced ham, fried flaked almonds or a few pinches of cumin to the paste. These sticks are delicious when served with an apéritif, accompanied by black or green olives.

Éperlans Frits
Deep-fried Smelts

Serves 6. Preparation and cooking: 10 min

★

○ **500g (18oz) smelts**
○ **juice of 1 lemon**
○ **5ml (1 tsp) parsley, roughly chopped**
○ **30g (1¼ oz) flour**
○ **1 litre (1¾ pints) oil for deep frying**

1. Heat the oil.
2. Wash and dry the smelts. Place the flour on a plate and roll the smelts in it. Then plunge them into hot oil and cook for 2 minutes. Drain well.
3. Mix the lemon juice with the parsley. Serve this sauce with the smelts.

Crevettes en Friture

Deep-fried Shrimps

Serves 6. Preparation and cooking: 5 min

★

○ **500g (18 oz) fresh shrimps (preferably live)**
○ **1 lemon**
○ **1 litre (1¾ pints) oil for deep frying**

1. Heat the oil. Wash the shrimps under running water. Drain.
2. When the oil is hot plunge the shrimps into it and fry for a few seconds. Drain. Serve with lemon quarters.

Serve the shrimps with slices of toasted and buttered rye bread.

Moules Frites

Deep-fried Mussels

Serves 4. Preparation: 20 min Cooking: 25 min

★

○ **2 litres (4½ lb) small mussels**
○ **1 egg, lightly beaten**
○ **200ml (7 fl oz) milk**
○ **15ml (1 tbls) olive oil**
○ **100g (4 oz) flour**
○ **1 lemon**
○ **5ml (1 tsp) parsley, roughly chopped**
○ **salt and pepper**
○ **240ml (9 fl oz) groundnut or olive oil for deep frying**

1. Scrub and wash the mussels well. Rinse a few times and drain.
2. Prepare the batter: in a bowl, mix the egg, milk and 15ml (1 tbls) olive oil. Season. Add the flour, and mix well with a wooden spoon until smooth. Let stand for 1 hour.
3. Place the mussels in a large saucepan over a high heat. When they open, drain them and remove from their shells.
4. Heat the oil in a frying pan.
5. Mix the mussels with the batter. With a spoon, drop them, one at a time, into the hot oil and fry for 10 minutes. Drain on absorbent paper. Serve hot with lemon wedges and parsley.

Croquettes de Morue

Salt Cod Croquettes

Serves 4-6. Preparation: 20 min Cooking: 35 min

★★

○ **400g (14 oz) filleted salt cod**
○ **400g (14 oz) potatoes**
○ **2 eggs**
○ **50g (2 oz) grated Gruyère cheese**
○ **30g (1¼ oz) butter**
○ **100ml (3½ fl oz) milk**
○ **2 pinches grated nutmeg**
○ **5ml (1 tsp) parsley, coarsely chopped**
○ **1 lemon**
○ **salt and pepper**
○ **30g (1¼ oz) flour**
○ **30g (1¼ oz) breadcrumbs**
○ **240ml (9 fl oz) oil for deep frying**

1. Soak the cod in cold water for 24 hours. Rinse well under running water. Drain.
2. Cook the potatoes for 25 minutes in salted water. Peel them.
3. In a saucepan filled with boiling water, poach the cod fillets for 2 minutes. Drain, remove the bones and skin and mash with a fork. Add the cooked potatoes and mash with the fish.
4. Place the cod mixture, butter, milk and nutmeg in a saucepan over a low heat. Season and mix well with a wooden spoon. Stir and cook until it thickens.
5. Remove from the heat and add the parsley and 1 egg. Mix and taste, adding more salt if necessary. Cover and let stand for 20 minutes.
6. Place the flour in one dish, a lightly beaten egg in another, and the breadcrumbs in a third.
7. Form the cod mixture into croquettes. Roll them in the flour, then in the egg and lastly in the bredcrumbs.
8. Heat the oil in a frying pan. Fry the croquettes in the hot oil for 1 to 2 minutes on each side. Drain on absorbent paper and serve with lemon wedges.

Croquettes de Crevettes

Serves 4. Preparation: 20 min Cooking: 25 min

Shrimp Croquettes

★ ★

- ○ **300g (10 oz) shelled shrimps**
- ○ **4 potatoes**
- ○ **30g (1¼ oz) butter**
- ○ **200ml (7 fl oz) milk**
- ○ **2 eggs**
- ○ **1 pinch grated nutmeg**
- ○ **30g (1¼ oz) breadcrumbs**
- ○ **30g (1¼ oz) flour**
- ○ **1 lemon**
- ○ **salt and pepper**
- ○ **1 litre (1¾ pints) oil for deep frying**

1. Peel the potatoes and cut into large pieces. Cook for 15 to 20 minutes in salted water. Drain and pass through the fine mesh of a vegetable mill. Add the butter, milk, nutmeg, 1 egg and the shrimps to the purée. Season and mix well. If the purée is too liquid, let it dry out over a fierce heat for a few seconds. Leave to stand for 15 minutes.
2. Place the flour in a dish, the breadcrumbs in another, and 1 egg, lightly beaten, in a third. Form the purée into small balls and dip each one in the flour, then in the egg and lastly in the breadcrumbs.
3. Heat the oil. Place the croquettes in a chip basket and plunge into the hot oil for 5 minutes. Drain on absorbent paper and serve with the lemon wedges.

Croquettes de Poulet

Serves 4. Preparation: 20 min Cooking: 10 min

Chicken Croquettes

★ ★

- ○ **4 cooked chicken breasts, chopped**
- ○ **200g (7 oz) minced steak**
- ○ **100g (4 oz) button mushrooms, cut into strips**
- ○ **1 onion, thinly sliced**
- ○ **5ml (1 tsp) parsley, coarsely chopped**
- ○ **30g (1¼ oz) flour**
- ○ **30g (1¼ oz) breadcrumbs**
- ○ **1 egg, lightly beaten**
- ○ **salt and pepper**
- ○ **240ml (9 fl oz) oil for deep frying**

1. Place the chicken, onion and mushrooms in a bowl. Add the minced steak and parsley. Season and mix well. Form into walnut-sized balls.
2. Place the flour in one dish, the breadcrumbs in another and the beaten egg in a third. Dip each ball in the flour, then in the egg and lastly in the breadcrumbs.
3. Heat the oil in a frying pan. Fry the croquettes in very hot oil for 10 minutes, turning them frequently so that they brown on all sides. Drain on absorbent paper and serve at once.

Croquettes de Gruyère

Serves 6. Preparation: 20 min Cooking: 10 min

Gruyère Croquettes

★ ★

- ○ **480ml (18 fl oz) milk**
- ○ **200g (7 oz) flour**
- ○ **6 eggs**
- ○ **150g (5 oz) grated Gruyère cheese**
- ○ **30g (1¼ oz) breadcrumbs**
- ○ **20g (¾ oz) butter**
- ○ **salt and pepper**
- ○ **240ml (9 fl oz) groundnut oil for deep frying**

1. Separate 3 eggs. In a bowl, mix the flour with 3 eggs and 3 egg yolks. Season and stir well until the mixture becomes paste-like.
2. Bring the milk to the boil. Place the paste in a saucepan and add the boiling milk. Cook over a low heat for 5 minutes, stirring constantly. Add the cheese and mix well.
3. Butter a baking sheet and pour the paste onto it, spreading it evenly to a thickness of 1½cm (slightly over ½ inch). Leave to cool.
4. Cut the paste into whatever shapes you choose: round, rectangular, square or triangular.
5. Beat the egg whites, and place the breadcrumbs on a plate. Dip each piece first in the egg whites, then in breadcrumbs.
6. In a frying pan, heat the oil and fry the croquettes for 2 minutes on each side.

Rissoles à la Viande

Serves 6. Preparation: 20 min Cooking: 40 min

Meat Fritters

★★

○ **250g (9 oz) flour**
○ **30ml (2 tbls) olive oil**
○ **juice of 1 lemon**
○ **1 large onion**
○ **20g (¾ oz) butter**
○ **500g (18 oz) minced steak**
○ **2 pinches grated nutmeg**
○ **1 clove, crushed**
○ **5ml (1 tsp) parsley, coarsely chopped**
○ **salt and pepper**
○ **1 litre (1¾ pints) oil for deep frying**

1. Sift the flour with 2 pinches of salt. Add the olive oil and mix with a fork. Add the lemon juice and 45ml (3 tbls) water. Mix well, cover and let stand for 1 hour.
2. Peel and finely chop the onion. Fry gently in the butter for 10 minutes over a low heat. Add the minced steak, nutmeg, crushed clove and parsley. Season, stir well and add 45ml (3 tbls) water. Cover and simmer for 15 minutes. Leave to cool.
3. Roll out the dough to a thickness of 3mm (⅛ inch). Cut into rounds approximately 12cm (5 inches) in diameter. Place 30ml (2 tbls) of the meat stuffing in the centre of each round, wet the edges, fold over and press the edges together well.
4. Heat the oil. Plunge the meat fritters into hot oil and cook for 15 minutes or until brown on both sides. Drain on absorbent paper and serve hot.

Beignets de Cervelle

Serves 6. Preparation: 20 min Cooking: 15 min

Brain Fritters

★★

○ **2 veal brains**
○ **5ml (1 tsp) parsley, coarsely chopped**
○ **1 lemon**
○ **salt**
○ **1 litre (1¾ pints) oil for deep frying**

For the dough:
○ **200g (7 oz) flour**
○ **40g (1¾ oz) butter**
○ **2 eggs**
○ **1 egg white**
○ **1 pinch salt**

1. Place the flour into a bowl and make a well in the centre. Melt the butter and add it to the flour with the 2 eggs, salt and 3 glasses of lukewarm water. Stir quickly. The batter should be perfectly smooth and have the consistency of a fairly thick sauce. Leave to stand for 1 hour. When it is time to use the batter, beat the egg white until stiff and fold it in gently.
2. Bring some salted water to the boil. Plunge the brains into boiling water for 5 minutes. Remove from the heat and drain. Remove the veins and slice.
3. Heat the oil. Dip the pieces of brain into the batter and, one at a time, using a spoon, plunge them into the hot oil. The fritters will brown in a few seconds. Drain on absorbent paper. Place on a serving dish and sprinkle with chopped parsley. Serve with lemon quarters.

Beignets de Pommes de Terre

Serves 6. Preparation: 15 min Cooking: 10 min

Potato Fritters

★

○ **5 eggs**
○ **1kg (2¼ lb) potatoes**
○ **5ml (1 tsp) chives, roughly chopped**
○ **salt and pepper**
○ **1 litre (1¾ pints) oil for deep frying**

1. Peel, wash and dry the potatoes.
2. Grate finely and drain to remove excess water.
3. Beat the eggs. Season and add the potatoes and chives. Mix well.
4. Heat the oil in a frying pan. Drop the potato mixture by spoonfuls into the hot oil and cook for 3 minutes on each side.
5. Remove the fritters and drain on absorbent paper. Serve hot.

Pâtés aux Épinards

Spinach Pasties

Serves 6. Preparation: 30 min Cooking: 40 min

★★

For the pastry:
○ **250g (9 oz) flour**
○ **30ml (2 tbls) olive oil**
○ **5ml (1 tsp) salt**
○ **1 egg**

For the filling:
○ **1kg (2¼ lb) fresh spinach**
○ **10g (½ oz) butter**
○ **2 eggs**
○ **1 carton fromage blanc or cream cheese**
○ **15ml (1 tbls) parsley, coarsely chopped**
○ **30g (1¼ oz) pistachio nuts, ground**
○ **salt and pepper**

For the glaze:
○ **1 egg yolk**

1. Prepare the pastry: beat the egg with a little water. Sift the flour and salt into a bowl. Fold in the oil and add the beaten egg, a little at a time, working with your hands. Knead the dough on a floured surface until it is firm and springy. If necessary, add a little flour. Cover the dough and let rest for 30 minutes.
2. Meanwhile, prepare the filling: remove the stalks from the spinach, wash and drain. Fry gently in the butter for 10 minutes, turning with a wooden spatula.
3. Drain the cheese, if necessary, and beat the 2 eggs.
4. On a board, place the drained spinach, parsley and pistachio nuts. Season and chop roughly.
5. Place these ingredients in a bowl, add the beaten eggs and cheese and mix well.
6. Preheat the oven to 200°C (400°F; gas mark 6).
7. Divide the dough equally into 4 balls and roll them out, one at a time, to a thickness of 3mm (⅛ inch). Cut the dough into small rectangles. You should get 12 of them. Place a small amount of the filling in the centre of each rectangle. Dampen the edges with a little water and fold over to enclose the filling. Press to seal. For the glaze, brush each pasty with the beaten egg mixed with a little water.
8. Place the pasties onto a baking sheet sprinkled with a little water. Bake for 30 minutes, checking from time to time. Serve at once.

Pâtés à la Viande et aux Pignons

Meat and Pine Nut Pasties

Serves 6. Preparation: 20 min Cooking: 1 hr

★★

For the pastry:
○ **200g (7 oz) flour**
○ **15ml (1 tbls) wine vinegar**
○ **30ml (2 tbls) olive oil**
○ **5ml (1 tsp) salt**
○ **1 egg**

For the filling:
○ **500g (18 oz) minced steak**
○ **5 fresh mint leaves**
○ **1 small onion**
○ **20g (¾ oz) pine nuts**
○ **10g (½ oz) currants**
○ **20g (¾ oz) butter**
○ **salt and pepper**

For the glaze:
○ **1 egg yolk**

1. In a bowl, mix the flour, egg, vinegar, oil and salt. The dough should be firm. Cover and let rest for 1 hour.
2. Prepare the filling: peel and chop the onion. Fry in butter for 10 minutes over a low heat. Add the minced steak, currants, mint leaves and pine nuts. Season. Stir with a wooden spoon and cook for 15 minutes over a low heat.
3. Preheat the oven to 200°C (400°F; gas mark 6).
4. Roll out the dough to a thickness of 3mm (⅛ inch) and divide it into squares of approximately 10cm (4 inches). Place 30-45ml (2-3 tbls) filling in the centre of each square. Wet the edges with a little water, and fold the 4 corners towards the centre. Press to seal and brush with a mixture of beaten egg yolk and a little water.
5. Sprinkle a little water on a baking sheet and place the pasties onto it. Bake for 35 minutes.

As a change, why not serve a selection of assorted small pasties with an apéritif or as the first course of a meal? Very simple to prepare, they can be filled with vegetables, meat or cheese and look attractive when glazed with an egg yolk and decorated using the blade of a knife.

Pâtés au Fromage
Cheese Pasties

Serves 6. Preparation: 15 min Cooking: 30 min

★★

For the pastry:
○ 200g (7 oz) flour
○ 30ml (2 tbls) olive oil
○ 5ml (1 tsp) salt
○ 1 egg

For the filling:
○ 500g (18 oz) fromage blanc
○ 1 egg
○ 1 pinch grated nutmeg
○ 15ml (1 tbls) parsley, coarsely chopped
○ salt and pepper

For the glaze:
○ 1 egg yolk

1. Prepare the pastry: beat the egg with a little water. Sift the flour and salt into a bowl. Fold in the oil and add the beaten egg gradually, working the dough with your hands. Knead the dough on a floured surface until it is firm and springy. If necessary, add a little more flour. Cover the dough and let rest for 30 minutes.
2. Prepare the filling: drain the fromage blanc, if necessary. Beat the eggs. Place the cheese in a bowl, and mix well with the egg, chopped parsley and grated nutmeg. Season and mix again.
3. Preheat the oven to 200°C (400°F; gas mark 6).
4. Roll out the dough to a thickness of 3mm (⅛ inch), and cut into rounds approximately 10cm (4 inches) in diameter. Place a small amount of filling in the centre of each round, wet the edges and fold over towards the middle. Seal. Brush with a mixture of beaten egg yolk and a little water. Place the pasties onto a baking sheet sprinkled with a little water, and bake for 30 minutes, checking to make sure they do not get too brown.

Tartelettes au Jambon et au Fromage
Ham and Cheese Tartlets

Serves 6. Preparation 10 min
Cooking: 20 min

★★

○ 200g (7 oz) grated Gruyère cheese
○ 200g (7 oz) cooked ham
○ 1 pinch cayenne pepper
○ 2 eggs
○ 20g (¾ oz) butter
○ 20g (¾ oz) flour
○ 200ml (7 fl oz) double cream

For the shortcrust pastry:
○ 200g (7 oz) flour
○ 100g (4 oz) butter
○ 1 pinch salt

1. Sift the flour into a bowl and make a well in the centre. Rub the diced butter into the flour with your fingertips, adding the salt.
2. Grease 6 tartlet tins and sprinkle with flour. Roll out the dough to a thickness of 5mm (¼ inch), cut into 6 circles and line each tin.
3. Preheat the oven to 230°C (450°F; gas mark 8).
4. Separate the eggs. Dice the ham. In a bowl, mix the egg yolks, cream, Gruyère, ham and cayenne pepper. Mix well, until smooth.
5. Fill each tartlet and bake for 20 minutes, checking from time to time.

Tarte au Roquefort et aux Noix
Roquefort and Walnut Tart

Serves 6. Preparation: 20 min
Cooking: 45 min

★★

○ 400g (14 oz) packet frozen puff pastry
○ 200g (7 oz) shelled walnuts
○ 200ml (7 fl oz) double cream
○ 200g (7 oz) Roquefort cheese
○ 130g (4½ oz) grated Gruyère cheese
○ 4 eggs
○ 1 pinch grated nutmeg
○ 10g (½ oz) butter
○ pepper

For the glaze:
○ 1 egg yolk

1. Thaw the pastry. Put aside 20 walnuts and finely chop the rest.
2. Mash the Roquefort to a purée with a fork, add the chopped walnuts and cream. Fold in the 4 eggs and grated Gruyère. Season with grated nutmeg and pepper.
3. Preheat the oven to 250°C (475°F; gas mark 9).
4. Roll out the pastry to a thickness of 5mm (¼ inch). Butter a pie dish, sprinkle it with flour and line it with the pastry. Prick the bottom and sides with a fork several times. Pour in the cheese mixture and brush the edges of the tart with a mixture of beaten egg yolk and a little water.
5. Bake 10 to 15 minutes, then garnish with the remaining walnuts. Reduce the heat to 170°C (325°F; gas mark 3) and bake for a further 30 minutes. Serve hot.

Friands aux Foies de Volaille (p73) ▶

Tarte à la Moutarde

Serves 4. Preparation: 15 min Cooking: 30 min

Mustard Tart

★

○ **400g (14 oz) frozen puff pastry**
○ **150g (5 oz) Gruyère cheese**
○ **5 tomatoes**
○ **120ml (4 fl oz) Dijon mustard**
○ **3 pinches oregano**
○ **10g (½ oz) butter**
○ **5g (¼ oz) flour**

1. Thaw the pastry.
2. Bring some water to the boil and immerse the tomatoes for 10 seconds. Peel, cut them into quarters and remove the seeds. Remove the crust of the cheese and cut it into strips.
3. Preheat the oven to 250°C (475°F; gas mark 9).
4. Roll out the pastry to a thickness of 5mm (¼ inch). Butter a pie dish and sprinkle it with flour, then line it with the pastry. Spread a layer of mustard (1cm/½ inch thick) on the bottom and cover with strips of Gruyère, then with tomato quarters. Sprinkle with oregano.
5. Bake for 30 minutes, checking from time to time to make sure it does not get too brown. Serve at once.

Tourte à la Tomme de Savoie

Serves 4. Preparation: 20 min
Cooking: 40 min

Cheese Tart

★ ★

○ **250g (9 oz) Tomme de Savoie cheese**
○ **2 eggs**
○ **100ml (3½ fl oz) white wine**
○ **30g (1¼ oz) grated Parmesan cheese**
○ **10g (½ oz) butter**
○ **10g (½ oz) flour**
○ **1 pinch grated nutmeg**
○ **salt and pepper**

For the shortcrust pastry:
○ **200g (7 oz) flour**
○ **100g (4 oz) softened butter**
○ **1 pinch salt**

1. In a bowl, sift together the flour and salt and make a well in the centre. Rub the diced butter into the flour with your fingertips, and gradually add 1 glass of water. The pastry should be homogeneous. Gather the dough into a ball and leave to stand for 1 hour.
2. Dice the cheese. Beat the eggs with the nutmeg and the white wine. Season.
3. Preheat the oven to 250°C (475°F; gas mark 9).
4. Butter and sprinkle a flan ring with flour. Roll out the dough to a thickness of 5mm (¼ inch) and line the pastry shell. Pour in the egg mixture and sprinkle with the diced and grated cheeses.
5. Roll the edges of the pastry into a rim of even thickness. Bake for 40 minutes and serve hot.

Tourte aux Légumes

Serves 6. Preparation: 25 min Cooking: 1 hr 20 min

Vegetable Tart

★ ★

○ **4 aubergines**
○ **1 onion**
○ **1 clove garlic**
○ **5 tomatoes**
○ **40g (1¾ oz) butter**
○ **5ml (1 tsp) parsley, coarsely chopped**
○ **30g (1¼ oz) grated Emmenthal cheese**
○ **salt and pepper**

For the pastry:
○ **400g (14 oz) flour**
○ **4 eggs**
○ **200ml (7 fl oz) milk**
○ **100ml (3½ fl oz) oil**
○ **1 pinch salt**
○ **60g (2¼ oz) butter**
○ **10ml (2 tsp) baking powder**

1. Place all the ingredients for the pastry in a bowl and mix with a wooden spoon until they form a smooth paste. Let rest while you prepare the vegetables.
2. Grill the aubergines on all sides for approximately 20 minutes. Leave to cool.
3. Preheat the oven to 170°C (325°F; gas mark 3).
4. Bring some water to the boil and immerse the tomatoes for 10 seconds. Drain, peel and remove the seeds. Peel the onion and clove of garlic, and chop them finely.
5. Melt 30g (1¼ oz) butter in a frying pan over a low heat, and gently fry the garlic and onion. Add the tomatoes, mash with a fork, season and cook uncovered for 10 minutes. Remove the skin of the aubergines, and add the flesh to the tomatoes. Cook for 5 minutes, add the parsley and grated cheese. Mix well.
6. Butter a soufflé dish and line it with two-thirds of the pastry. Fill with the vegetable mixture and cover with the remaining pastry. Bake for approximately 40 minutes and serve hot.

Friands aux Foies de Volaille

Chicken Liver Puffs

Serves 6. Preparation: 20 min
Cooking: 35 min
★★

○ **400g (14 oz) frozen puff pastry**
○ **150g (5 oz) chicken livers**
○ **150g (5 oz) pork sausagemeat**
○ **5ml (1 tbls) cognac**
○ **15 sprigs parsley, coarsely chopped**
○ **1 clove garlic**
○ **30g (1¼ oz) butter**
○ **salt and pepper**

For the glaze:
○ **1 egg yolk**

1. Thaw the pastry.
2. Prepare the filling: peel and chop the garlic finely. Coarsely chop the chicken livers. Melt the butter in a frying pan over a medium heat and fry the livers gently. Add the sausagemeat and garlic. Season and stir with a wooden spoon. Cook for 15 minutes. Pour over the cognac and set alight. Remove from the heat and add the parsley.
3. Preheat the oven to 230°C (450°F; gas mark 8).
4. Roll out the pastry to a thickness of 5mm (¼ inch) and cut it into 12 squares. Place a small amount of the filling in the centre of each square and fold the corners towards the middle. Brush the puffs with a mixture of beaten egg yolk and a little water.
5. Sprinkle a baking sheet with water and place the chicken liver puffs onto it. Bake for 20 minutes, checking occasionally, to make sure they do not get too brown.

Friands au Jambon

Ham Puffs

Serves 4. Preparation: 20 min Cooking: 30 min
★★

○ **400g (14 oz) frozen puff pastry**
○ **1 onion**
○ **150g (5 oz) cooked ham**
○ **25g (1 oz) butter**
○ **60ml (4 tbls) double cream**
○ **100g (4 oz) Tomme de Savoie cheese**
○ **salt and pepper**

For the glaze:
○ **1 egg yolk**

1. Thaw the pastry. Peel and chop the onion. Chop the ham. Melt the butter in a frying pan and gently fry the onion and ham over a low heat, stirring occasionally. Add the cream and cook, uncovered, for 5 minutes. Season, remove from the heat and leave to cool.
2. Dice the cheese and add it to the mixture in the frying pan.
3. Preheat the oven to 230°C (450°F; gas mark 8).
4. On a floured surface, roll out the pastry to a thickness of 3mm (⅛ inch). Divide it into 8 squares and place one-quarter of the filling in the centre of each of 4 squares. Wet the edges with a little water and cover each with one of the 4 remaining squares. Press the edges firmly together. Brush with the egg yolk beaten with a little water to glaze.
5. Sprinkle a baking sheet with water and place the puffs on it. Bake for 20 minutes, checking from time to time to make sure they do not get too brown. Serve hot.

Vol-au-Vent Breton

Vol-au-Vent Breton Style

Serves 4. Preparation and cooking: 50 min
★★

○ **1 large vol-au-vent**
○ **200g (7 oz) cushion of veal**
○ **200g (7 oz) chicken breasts**
○ **120ml (4 fl oz) white wine**
○ **30g (1¼ oz) flour**
○ **1 chicken stock cube**
○ **200ml (7 fl oz) double cream**
○ **150g (5 oz) button mushrooms, cut into strips**
○ **90g (3¾ oz) butter**
○ **salt and pepper**

1. Thaw and bake the vol-au-vent, if frozen. Dice the veal and chicken, and gently fry with the mushrooms in 30g (1¼ oz) butter over a low heat, until brown. Season and add the white wine, and cook for 15 minutes.
2. Preheat the oven to 200°C (400°F; gas mark 6).
3. Dissolve the stock cube in 240ml (9 fl oz) water. In a saucepan, melt 60g (2½ oz) butter. Add the flour and stir with a wooden spoon. Add the chicken stock, a little at a time, stirring constantly. Add the cream, season, and cook for 10 minutes, stirring constantly to ensure that the sauce thickens properly. Add the sauce to the meat, mix gently and fill the vol-au-vent case with the mixture. Bake for 15 minutes.

Vol-au-Vent aux Rognons

Serves 4. Preparation and cooking: 50 min

Kidney Vol-au-Vent

★★

○ 4 individual vol-au-vent
○ 2 pig's kidneys
○ 1 veal kidney
○ 15ml (1 tbls) cognac
○ 15ml (1 tbls) white wine
○ 300g (10 oz) button
   mushrooms
○ 200ml (7 fl oz) double cream
○ 80g (3¼ oz) butter
○ salt and pepper

For the white sauce (béchamel):
○ 20g (¾ oz) butter
○ 10g (½ oz) flour
○ 60ml (2 fl oz) milk
○ salt and pepper

1. Thaw and bake the vol-au-vent, if frozen. Halve the kidneys, remove the skin and fat. Wipe dry and cut them into slices. Blanch for 5 minutes in boiling water and drain.
2. Cut the earthy base from the mushrooms, wash under running water and cut into strips.
3. Preheat the oven to 230°C (450°F; gas mark 8).
4. Melt 30g (1¼ oz) of butter in a frying pan and fry the kidneys over a high heat. When they have given out all their juices, remove from the heat and drain away the cooking juices. Place the frying pan back on the heat and deglaze with the cognac. Add the cream and white wine, and let reduce over a low heat for 10 minutes.
5. In another frying pan, fry the mushrooms in 50g (2 oz) butter for 10 minutes, stirring with a wooden spatula. Add the mushrooms and kidneys to the cream sauce and cook for a few more minutes.
6. Fill each vol-au-vent with the kidney mixture and bake for 5 minutes.
7. Meanwhile, melt the butter in a saucepan over a low heat. Add the flour and stir well but do not let it brown. Add the cold milk, stirring constantly with a wooden spoon. Season.
8. Take the vol-au-vent from the oven, top each with a spoonful of béchamel, and serve at once.

To deglaze is to add a liquid (cognac, in this recipe) to a pan in which food has previously been cooked, then bring quickly to a boil, scraping up the crusty bits at the bottom of the pan with a wooden spoon.

Bouchées aux Huîtres

Serves 6. Preparation: 25 min Cooking: 40 min

Oyster Vol-au-vent

★★★

○ 6 individual vol-au-vent
○ 4 dozen oysters
○ 150g (5 oz) butter mushrooms
○ 100g (4 oz) prawns
○ 60ml (4 tbls) double cream
○ 25g (1 oz) flour
○ juice of 1 lemon
○ 60g (2¼ oz) butter
○ 120ml (4 fl oz) milk
○ 120ml (4 fl oz) white wine
○ 1 onion, peeled
○ 1 bouquet garni consisting of:
   1 sprig thyme, 2 bay leaves

1. Thaw and bake the vol-au-vent, if frozen. Open the oysters, pour their juices into a saucepan, and bring to the boil. Blanch the oysters for 1 minute. Strain the cooking juices through a fine sieve. Put the oysters aside.
2. Preheat the oven to 230°C (450°F; gas mark 8).
3. Shell the prawns and put aside. Put the shells of the prawns and the juice of the oysters in a saucepan, together with the white wine, bouquet garni and onion. Simmer for 15 minutes. Strain through a fine sieve and put aside.
4. Cut the earthy base from the mushrooms and wash under running water. In a saucepan, over a low heat, melt 30g (1¼ oz) butter, add the mushrooms and lemon juice and cook slowly for 15 minutes.
5. In another saucepan, melt the remaining butter, sprinkle in the flour, and stir over a low heat. Then add the milk, a little at a time, together with the reserved stock. Stir with a wooden spoon until it thickens. Remove from the heat and add 60ml (4 tbls) cream. Stir well, add the oysters, prawns and mushrooms, and heat.
6. Fill the vol-au-vent cases with the mixture and bake for 2 minutes. Serve at once.

Vol-au-vent are delicious when filled with scallops, sole fillets, mussels, sweetbreads or brains in a béchamel, to which you can add Madeira or lemon juice.

Feuilleté au Jambon

Ham in Puff Pastry

Serves 4. Preparation: 20 min Cooking: 1 hr 20 min

★ ★

- ○ **400g (14 oz) frozen puff pastry**
- ○ **8 thin slices cooked ham**
- ○ **400g (14 oz) button mushrooms**
- ○ **2 large onions**
- ○ **1 large shallot**
- ○ **60g (2¼ oz) butter**
- ○ **2 pinches grated nutmeg**
- ○ **60g (2¼ oz) grated Gruyère cheese**
- ○ **15ml (1 tbls) double cream**
- ○ **salt and pepper**

For the white sauce (béchamel):
- ○ **240ml (9 fl oz) milk**
- ○ **50g (2 oz) butter**
- ○ **30g (1¼ oz) flour**
- ○ **salt and pepper**

For the glaze:
- ○ **1 egg yolk**

1. Thaw the pastry. Divide it into 2 and roll out each piece to a thickness of 3mm (⅛ inch). With a round baking tin, mark out a circle on each piece of pastry. Sprinkle a baking sheet with water and place one circle of pastry on it.
2. Prepare the béchamel: melt the butter in a saucepan over a low heat and stir in the flour, making sure it does not brown. Add the cold milk a little at a time, stirring constantly with a wooden spoon, and cook for 15 minutes. Season.
3. Remove from heat, and add the nutmeg, cheese and cream. Season and mix well.
4. Dice the ham. Cut the earthy base from the mushrooms, wash under running water and cut into strips. Peel the onions and shallot, and chop very finely.
5. Melt the butter in a frying pan over a low heat, and fry the shallot and onions for 10 minutes. Add the diced ham and mushroom strips. Turn the heat up and fry the ingredients for 10 minutes, stirring constantly with a wooden spatula, until most of the liquid has evaporated.
6. Preheat the oven to 230°C (450°F; gas mark 8).
7. Pour the ingredients from the frying pan into a bowl and slowly fold in the white sauce. Place this filling onto the pastry on the baking sheet. Dampen the edges with a little water and cover with the other circle of pastry. Press the edges together to seal. Brush the top with the egg yolk beaten with a little water to glaze. Bake for 20 minutes, then turn the heat down to 170°C (325°F; gas mark 3) and cook for a further 25 minutes.

Feuilleté Napolitain

Neapolitan Puffs

Serves 4. Preparation: 15 min Cooking: 30 min

★

- ○ **400g (14 oz) frozen puff pastry**
- ○ **2 large tomatoes**
- ○ **8 black olives, stoned**
- ○ **1 large mozzarella cheese**
- ○ **small tin of anchovies in oil**
- ○ **1 egg yolk**

1. Thaw the pastry.
2. Halve the tomatoes, remove the seeds and slice them. Slice the mozzarella. Drain the anchovies.
3. Preheat the oven to 200°C (400°F; gas mark 6).
4. Divide the pastry into 2 pieces. Roll out each one to a thickness of 3mm (⅛ inch) and cut 4 rounds from each. On four of the rounds, place a slice of mozzarella, covered with a slice of tomato, 2 olives and 1 anchovy fillet. Wet the edges with a little water and top with the remaining 4 rounds. Press the edges together to seal.
5. Brush each puff with egg yolk beaten with a little water to glaze. Place them on a baking sheet sprinkled with a little water and bake for approximately 30 minutes.

Certain pasties made of puff pastry may be deep fried instead of being baked. This method is best for pasties with spicy or highly seasoned fillings, such as anchovy paste with chervil, or soft cheese and chives. An egg glaze is not necessary.

Crêpes au Fromage

Cheese Pancakes

Serves 4-6. Preparation: 10 min Cooking: 40 min

★★

For the pancake batter:
- ○ **200g (7 oz) flour**
- ○ **½ litre (18 fl oz) milk**
- ○ **2 eggs**
- ○ **15ml (1 tbls) oil**
- ○ **1 pinch salt**

For the filling:
- ○ **300g (11 oz) Comté cheese (or substitute Gruyère)**
- ○ **200ml (7 fl oz) double cream**
- ○ **4 pinches grated nutmeg**
- ○ **15ml (1 tbls) oil**
- ○ **salt and pepper**

1. Prepare the pancake batter: sift the flour into a bowl. Make a well in the centre and break the eggs into it, then add the oil, pinch of salt and 60ml (2 fl oz) milk. Beat vigorously with a wooden spoon until smooth. Stir in the remaining milk a little at a time. Let rest for 1 hour.
2. Remove the crust of the cheese and cut it into strips.
3. Preheat the oven to 140°C (275°F; gas mark 1).
4. Cook the pancakes: heat the oil in a frying pan, and, when the pan is very hot, pour in just enough batter to cover the base of the pan thinly. Cook each pancake, turning to cook both sides, for 3 minutes. Rub the frying pan with oil when necessary. Fill the pancakes with the strips of cheese and fold them over to form a triangle. Leave them on the heat for a few seconds so that the cheese melts. As soon as each pancake is ready, place in an ovenproof dish and keep warm in the oven, leaving the door ajar.
5. Beat the cream with a whisk, add the grated nutmeg. Season and place in the freezer for 2 minutes. Serve the very cold cream with the hot pancakes.

Crêpes au Fromage et aux Épinards

Cheese and Spinach Pancakes

Serves 5. Preparation: 15 min
Cooking: 30 min

★★

For the pancake batter:
- ○ **200g (7 oz) flour**
- ○ **½ litre (18 fl oz) milk**
- ○ **2 eggs**
- ○ **15ml (1 tbls) oil**
- ○ **1 pinch salt**

For the filling:
- ○ **500g (18 oz) fromage blanc or cream cheese**
- ○ **200g (7 oz) fresh spinach**
- ○ **15ml (1 tbls) coarsely chopped herbs: tarragon, parsley, chervil and chives**
- ○ **1 lemon**
- ○ **15ml (1 tbls) oil**
- ○ **20g (¾ oz) butter**
- ○ **salt and pepper**

1. Prepare the pancake batter: sift the flour into a bowl, make a well in the centre and break the eggs into the middle. Add the oil, pinch of salt and 60ml (2 fl oz) milk. Beat vigorously with a wooden spoon until smooth. Add the remaining milk a little at a time. Let rest for 1 hour.
2. Bring some salted water to the boil. Remove the stalks from the spinach, wash and drain the leaves, and plunge them into the boiling water. Cook for 10 minutes. Drain well.
3. Chop the spinach. Beat the fromage blanc with a whisk, then mix in the chopped spinach and herbs. Season.
4. Preheat the oven to 200°C (400°F; gas mark 6).
5. Cook the pancakes: heat the oil in a frying pan. When the oil is hot, pour in just enough batter to cover the base of the pan thinly. Turn or toss the pancake when brown. Repeat, rubbing the pan with oil whenever necessary.
6. Place the pancakes on a plate, spread each one with the fromage blanc mixture and roll them up. Place them in an ovenproof dish. Dot with knobs of butter and cook in the oven for 3 to 5 minutes. Serve with lemon slices.

Stuffed pancakes can be a pleasant surprise: there are so many fillings to choose from. Here are just a few examples for you to try: chopped chicken livers fried with shallots and mushrooms in white wine; diced ham sautéed with black olives, parsley and a beaten egg; fish or shellfish bound with a béchamel. Just cook the pancakes and stuff with your favourite filling.

Crêpes Farcies

Serves 4. Preparation: 20 min Cooking: 15 min

Stuffed Pancakes

★★

- ○ **8 pancakes made with buckwheat flour**
- ○ **3 slices of ham (Bayonne style)**
- ○ **100g (4 oz) Comté cheese (or substitute Gruyère), grated**
- ○ **200ml (7 fl oz) double cream**
- ○ **400g (14 oz) canned asparagus tips**
- ○ **half a grated nutmeg**
- ○ **20g (¾ oz) butter**
- ○ **salt and pepper**

1. Bring 1 litre (1¾ pints) water to the boil. Open the asparagus tins, rinse the tips in a colander and drain. Plunge them in the boiling water for 2 seconds and drain.
2. Meanwhile, remove the rind of the ham, put the slices on top of each other and cut into squares.
3. In a bowl, place the ham squares, cream, grated cheese (reserving a little to sprinkle over the pancakes) and nutmeg. Season with pepper and a little salt.
4. Preheat the oven to 230°C (450°F; gas mark 8).
5. Place the asparagus tips in a bowl and mix gently with the ham and cheese mixture, using a wooden spoon, until the mixture is smooth.
6. Fill each pancake with some stuffing and roll them up.
7. In a lightly buttered ovenproof dish, place the pancakes and dot with knobs of butter and the remaining cheese. Cook in the oven for 15 minutes, until the cheese melts and starts to brown, checking from time to time.

Croustades Arc-en-Ciel

Serves 6. Preparation: 20 min Cooking: 35 min

Prawn Tartlets

★★

- ○ **300g (10 oz) prawns**
- ○ **2 carrots**
- ○ **2 potatoes**
- ○ **100g (4 oz) peas**
- ○ **2 gherkins**
- ○ **45ml (3 tbls) mayonnaise**
- ○ **12 black olives, stoned**
- ○ **10g (½ oz) butter**
- ○ **10g (½ oz) flour**

For the shortcrust pastry:
- ○ **200g (7 oz) flour**
- ○ **100g (4 oz) butter**
- ○ **1 pinch salt**

1. Prepare the pastry: in a bowl, sift the flour and make a well in the centre. Add the salt and the diced butter. Rub in with your fingertips, adding 1 glass of water, a little at a time. The mixture should be homogeneous. Gather the pastry into a ball and let rest for 1 hour.
2. Preheat the oven to 200°C (400°F; gas mark 6). Roll out the pastry on a floured surface. Divide it into 6 small rounds and line 6 buttered and floured tartlet moulds. Bake for 20 minutes.
3. Meanwhile, shell the prawns and put 6 of them aside. Peel the carrots and potatoes, wash and cut them into thin strips. Shell the peas. Cook the vegetables in salted water for 15 minutes. Drain. Slice the gherkins.
4. In a bowl, mix the mayonnaise with the vegetables, prawns and gherkins.
5. When the tartlets are cooked, fill them with the mixture and garnish with 1 prawn and 2 black olives.

Buckwheat flour may be substituted for white flour when making pancakes with savoury fillings. Try making a 'cake' of 10 buckwheat pancakes, stacked on top of each other, with a layer of asparagus, sorrel or spinach in cream between each pancake. Another excellent idea for a starter is fried eggs topping buckwheat pancakes.

Wines: the Finishing Touch

Nowadays excellent quality table wines are within the reach of everyone, though you should expect to pay more for a good vintage wine from one of the famous vineyards, such as Nuits-St-Georges or Schloss Johannisberg Riesling. When buying French wine, look for the *Appellation Côntrolée* label, which is a guarantee of quality.

Below is a guide to the wines that go best with certain foods, but there are no absolute *rules* about which wine to serve with what food – in the end it is your palate that must decide. For a large, formal meal, certain wines traditionally follow each other through the menu and you could serve three or even four wines at one meal. In this case, it is usual to serve dry sherry with the soup, dry white wine with the fish course, claret or burgundy with the meat or game and a white dessert wine or medium sweet champagne with the dessert. For cheese, your guests would return to the claret or burgundy. Certain foods kill the flavour of wine and should therefore be avoided if you are planning to serve wine with the meal. Mint sauce, for example, or any salad with a strong vinaigrette dressing, will destroy the taste of the wine.

Remember that red wines are generally served *chambré*, or at room temperature, to bring out the flavour. Draw the cork at least three or four hours before you plan to drink the wine and let the bottle stand in the kitchen or a warm room. (Never be tempted into putting the bottle in hot water or in front of the fire – the flavour will be ruined.) The exception to the *chambré* rule is Beaujolais, which can be served cool – some people even serve it chilled. White or rosé wines are usually served chilled – the easiest way is to put them in the fridge an hour before serving, or plunge them into an ice bucket, if you have one. Champagne should also be served well chilled and is generally brought to the table in an ice bucket.

Wines to Serve with Food

Oysters, shellfish	Chablis, dry Moselle, Champagne
Fried or grilled fish	Dry Graves, Moselle, Hock, Rosé, Blanc de Blanc
Fish with sauces	Riesling, Pouilly-Fuissé, Chablis
Veal, pork or chicken dishes (served simply)	Rosé, Riesling, a light red wine such as Beaujolais
Chicken or pork served with a rich sauce	Claret, Côte de Rhône, Médoc
Rich meat dishes, steaks, game	Red Burgundy, Rioja, Red Chianti
Lamb or duck	Claret, Beaujolais
Desserts and puddings	White Bordeaux, Sauternes, Entre Deux Mers
Cheese	Burgundy, Rioja, Cabernet Sauvignon

This edition published 1992 by Wordsworth Editions Ltd, 8b East Street, Ware, Hertfordshire.

Copyright © Wordsworth Editions Ltd 1992.

Designed by Tony Selina, The Old Goat Graphic Company, London, England.

ISBN 1-85326-978-6

Printed and bound in Hong Kong by South China Printing Company.